Hockey
Goaltending
for Young Players

Hockey Goaltending

for *Young Players*

AN INSTRUCTIONAL GUIDE

François Allaire

KEY PORTER BOOKS

First published in Quebec by Les Éditions de l'Homme, a division of the Sogides Group
Published in Canada in 1997 by Key Porter Books

Canadian Cataloguing in Publication Data

Allaire, François, 1955–
    Hockey goaltending for young players : an instructional guide

Translation of: Devenir gardien de but au hockey.
ISBN: 1-55013-895-2

1. Hockey – Goalkeeping.   2. Hockey – Training.   I. Title.

GV848.76.A4413 1997a   796.962'27   C97-931311-2

The publisher gratefully acknowledges the support of the Canada Council for the Arts and the Ontario Arts Council for its publishing program.

Key Porter Books Limited
70 The Esplanade
Toronto, Ontario
Canada M5E 1R2

Design and page layout: Ginette Brassard
Photographs: Stéphanie Brisson
Exercise illustrations: Michel Fleury and John Lightfoot
Translation: Brenda O'Brien
Material supplied by Koho Canada.

Printed and bound in Canada

97 98 99 00 6 5 4 3 2 1

Contents

G U I D E
T O   S Y M B O L S

Symbols for offense players

Forward	◯
Defenseman	△
Forward movement	⟶
Backward movement	∿∿∿∿
Movement with puck	∼∼⟶
Pass	- - - →
Shot on goal	⟹

Symbols for goaltenders

Goaltender in basic
standing position

Goaltender in basic
crouching position

Goaltender in basic
kneeling position

Forward movement
in basic standing position

Backward movement
in basic standing position

Forward movement
in basic crouching position

Backward movement
in basic crouching position

Movement to the right in basic standing
position, skates parallel

Movement to the left in basic standing position,
skates parallel

T-push to the right

T-push to the left

Stop   //

Puck immobilization

Kneeling-standing movement

Goalie observing the puck

Puck handling

Pass

Shooting the puck to the right

Shooting the puck to the left

Miscellaneous symbols

Coach   E

Cone   X

Puck (or ball)   ●

Net

Stick

Introduction

One of the biggest challenges for a minor hockey coach is to train his young goalies at the same pace as the other players on the team.

The coach's limited experience with goalies, the lack of time during training sessions, and the scarcity of documentation on goaltending techniques make the young beginner goalie different from other team members. This is why this publication outlines a development plan specifically for beginner goalies.

What is a development plan? It's simply an overall plan that extends over a four-year period.

The plan covers skating techniques, basic technical moves, the physical attributes to develop off the ice, evaluation methods, and several other topics crucial to the proper development of a beginner goalie.

The topics examined in the last chapter are a summary of the things a goaltending coach should teach his goalies during their stay in the beginner category (9 to 12 years old).

However, training methods (number of repetitions, rate at which techniques are introduced, the order in which the various techniques are taught, the variety of exercises used, etc.) are left to the coach's discretion.

The coach's only obligation is to teach young goalies as many of the elements contained in this development plan as possible before they reach the age of 12. At that age, goalies reach the intermediate stage.

Constantly in close contact with goaltenders, the coach is the person in the best position to plan specific training for the goalies for whom he has responsibility.

It is important to note that, at the intermediate stage, other technical skills and other physical and mental qualities are needed to succeed as a goalie.

This publication is ideal for individuals (coaches, parents, goalies) involved with teams in the Novice, Atom, and Pee-Wee categories since it provides a detailed development plan (on-ice, off-ice, special exercises, etc.) and it also meets the needs of anyone involved in teams which fall into categories involving higher-caliber play, with chapters on observation, communication, correction, the roles of a goaltending coach, etc.

Many young goalies have extraordinary talent. By teaching them crucial concepts and specific exercises early in their careers, coaches can make sure that young goalies get more fun from their favorite sport and achieve higher levels of efficiency.

This book contains:
A development plan for the beginner goalie

Beginner
Intermediate
Advanced

SUMMARY

1. An outline of the goalie's development stages.

2. An outline of the characteristics which make a beginner goalie different from a goalie who has gone beyond the beginner stage.

3. The hockey season in graphic form and what it involves.

4. The goalie development plan in graphic form and what it involves.

	1	2	3	4
Period	Preseason	Season	Playoffs	Postseason
Month	J A	S O N D J F	M A	M J
A **On-Ice** **training**		1 — Skating techniques /————————/ 2 — Basic techniques / 3 — On-ice evaluation /——/ /——/ /——/	/	
B **Off-ice** **training**	I — Off-ice training sessions /———————————————/ II — Group /———————/ sports			II — Group /————————/ sports
		IV — Off-ice evaluation /——/ /——/ /——/		III — Individual /————————/ sports

There are three very specific stages in the life of a goalie who starts to play at age nine and tends goals until he reaches adulthood:

1st: beginner goalie (from 9 to 12 years old);
2nd: intermediate goalie (from 13 to 16 years old);
3rd: advanced goalie (17 years old and over).

Each stage involves a certain number of very specific elements that must be mastered to go on to the next stage.

Therefore, the beginner goalie's development must be planned. The best means to achieve this objective is to build a development plan extending over approximately four years and based on each goalie's ability.

The development process aims at reducing the luck factor to a minimum and developing as specifically as possible each of the major aspects of the role played by a beginner goalie, namely:

1. skating techniques (Chapter 1);
2. basic techniques (Chapter 2);
3. the physical attributes crucial to a goalie's work (Chapter 4).

Learning and practicing these techniques and physical qualities enables a young person (who is starting to play in the net) to reach the level of skill needed to train efficiently for the next stage

The following table shows the characteristics of a beginner goalie and the characteristics of a goalie who has completed the beginner stage.

Characteristics of a beginner goalie	Characteristics of a goalie who has completed of the beginner stage

— Difficulty skating
  • poor balance (falls often)
  • can't keep up with the pace of the game
	— Can skate easily and quickly both inside and outside his goal

— Has mastered very few basic techniques
  • uncoordinated movements
  • difficulty carrying out different technical moves
  • mistakes in choosing the basic techniques to use
	— Has mastered most basic techniques needed to tend goal and uses them correctly

— Difficulty with puck-stopping techniques
  • difficulty judging the shots directed at him
  • gives up a high number of rebounds
  • often uses the wrong piece of equipment
	— Is effective at stopping most shots directed toward him

— Analyzes game situations poorly • little experience and background	— Analyzes game situations well and makes adjustments accordingly

— Lacks confidence
  • stays deep in his net
  • often crouches down on the ice
	— Is more sure of himself and now has his own personal style

— Difficulty with equipment
  • too big or too heavy
  • doesn't provide enough protection
	— Can select equipment suited to his needs and abilities

— Generally acceptable physical fitness level	— Has the physical fitness level needed for more rigorous training

1. The hockey season in graphic form

Table I shows a season within a development plan. The periods that make up a hockey season are listed horizontally, with the corresponding months. The two types of training needed to develop a beginner goalie, both on the ice and off the ice, appear vertically.

Seasons

Table I

	1	2	3	4
Period	Preseason	Season	Playoffs	Postseason
Month	J A	S O N D J F	M A	M J
A On-ice training				
B Off-ice training				

Each season is divided into four very specific periods.

1. In the preseason (July and August), the objective is to prepare the goalie physically and psychologically for the upcoming season.
2. During the season itself (September to mid February), the objective is to develop the beginner goalie's skills while maintaining or improving his physical fitness level.
3. During the playoffs (mid February to late April), the objective is to prepare the beginner goalie to face the opposing teams he will play against.
4. In the postseason (May and June), the objective is to allow time for physical and psychological recuperation, while maintaining the beginner goalie in good overall physical condition.

2. The goalie development plan in detailed graphic form

For each of these four periods in the season, the beginner goalie must practice certain elements, both on and off the ice.

In the following table, these elements are represented by lines that indicate how long they should be practiced.

For example, skating techniques should be included in on-ice training sessions from early September to late February. And so on for each of the lines included in the table.

Arabic numerals indicate the order of importance of each element in on-ice training. Roman numerals are used for the same purpose, in off-ice training sessions.

Table II

	1	2	3	4
Period	Preseason	Season	Playoffs	Postseason
Month	J A	S O N D J F	M A	M J
A **On-ice** **training**		1 — Skating techniques ⊢——————————⟋ 2 — Basic techniques ⊢————————————⟋ 3 — On-ice evaluation ⊢—⟋ ⊢—⟋ ⊢—⟋		
B **Off-ice** **training**	II — Group sports ⊢——⟋	I — Off-ice training sessions ⊢——————————⟋ IV — Off-ice evaluation ⊢—⟋ ⊢—⟋ ⊢—⟋		II — Group sports ⊢———————⟋ III — Individual sports ⊢———————⟋

On the following pages, each of the various elements included in each of the periods of the development plan for beginner goalies is described.

On-Ice Training

On-ice training is the largest and best-known part of a coach's duties. The training includes:

— skating techniques;
— basic techniques;
— on-ice evaluation.

To ensure the best possible training for young beginner goalies, it is important to establish certain very specific rules on the ideal frequency of on-ice training sessions.

	1	2	3	4
Period	Preseason	Season	Playoffs	Postseason
Month	J A	S O N D J F	M A	M J
A On-Ice training	F*: nil	F*: 3 times/week (90 minutes per training session) 1 or 2 games 1 or 2 training sessions (1 with the team; 1 with the municipality goalie's school)	F*: 4 times/week (90 minutes per training session) 2 or 3 games 1 or 2 training sessions with the team	F*: nil
B Off-ice training				

F*: Ideal frequency of on-ice training for goalies in each of the various periods of a hockey season.

CHAPTER
1

SKATING
TECHNIQUES

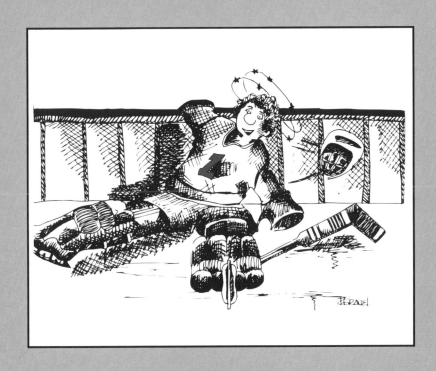

SUMMARY

1. Demonstrate the importance of SKATING for a beginner goalie.
2. Describe what good SKATING SKILLS can do for a beginner goalie.
3. Describe each of the SKATING TECHNIQUES a beginner goalie needs.

	1	2	3	4
Period	Preseason	Season	Playoffs	Postseason
Month	J A	S O N D J F	M A	M J
A On-ice training		1 — Skating techniques /————/		
B Off-ice training				

Skating has long been recognized as the most important technical aspect of hockey. And as a player, the goalie is no exception to the rule. In fact, he is more subject to it than any of his counterparts. After all, isn't he on the ice for the entire duration of each game?

The performance level a beginner goalie can reach is based on his ability to master skating techniques. A young goalie who learns to skate properly can achieve:

— good balance on skates;
— speed and agility on the ice, two attributes needed for easy and precise moves.

Among other things, these qualities will make it possible for him:

— to increase his speed of movement;
— to follow the puck more efficiently;
— to boost his confidence and motivation;
— to move out of his net;
— to reduce fatigue during games and practice sessions;
— to increase his ability to learn basic techniques specific to the role of a goalie.

Hard work and correct teaching of skating techniques will make it possible for any young goalie to achieve precisely the level of performance described above. Therefore, it is important for the young goalie to skate with the rest of his team during training sessions and at every possible opportunity that presents itself: free skate times, hockey school, skating at an outdoor rinks, etc.

During training sessions, the coach should require as much quality in technical moves from the goalie as he does from the rest of the team's players. On the other hand, the goalie's skating will be less intense and slower because of the weight of his equipment.

The following pages explain in detail each of the skating techniques a beginner goalie needs. All technical moves should be taught during the team's skating practices.

Like any other player on the team, the goalie should be involved in every skating practice. Since the goalie should be doing the same work as other players, this chapter does not include skating exercises designed specifically for goalies.

In addition, most coaches are capable of creating their own exercises to help players learn the skating techniques described on the following pages.

Forward start

1. The goalie is standing. Skates are a shoulder-width apart.
2. The torso and knees are slightly bent. The head is facing front.
3. At the outset, the push skate opens out and the body is thrown off balance toward the front.
4. Weight is shifted over the push skate and a strong push is produced by the hip and knee of the push leg.
5. The first three or four strides are short and quick.

Side start*

1. The goalie is standing. At the outset, the head is facing a given direction and the body is thrown off balance in the same direction.
2. The shoulders rotate in the same direction and the outside leg crosses over the inside leg. At this point the outside leg pushes.
3. The blade of the cross skate is placed perpendicular to the desired direction. The inside leg is brought forward again to begin the next push. At this point, the movement is identical to the movement in the forward start (see points 3, 4, 5 above).

* This technique should be practiced from the right side and from the left side.

Forward skating

1. After a start, forward skating requires that the body's weight be on the push skate at the start of each stride.
2. The stride begins with a strong push from the hip and knee, directed toward the side and back.
3. Shoulders are perpendicular to the desired direction, the body is bent forward and the knee is positioned ahead of the tip of the skate during the gliding stage.

Stopping on an outside skate*

1. Skating forward, the goalie rotates his hips to place the blade of his outside skate perpendicular to his direction.
2. The body's weight rests on the front part of the blade, and the knee of the same leg is bent to absorb part of the shock.
3. The inside leg is swung back and is not involved in the stop. The body is bent forward and the stick is pointed in the same direction.
4. When the stop is complete, the goalie can easily initiate a backward start to return to the basic position in his net.

* This technique should be practiced from the right side and from the left side.

Forward crossover stride*

1. The head and shoulders are turned to the center of the crease. The body is bent forward.
2. The body's weight is on the inside skate, which pushs to the outside as the outside skate crosses over to become the inside skate.
3. The front of the blades is used to push. Legs cross alternately.

---

* This technique should be practiced from the right side and from the left side.

Pivot (forward skating to backward skating)*

1. The skater straightens the knees and torso slightly to bring skates closer together. The body's weight is placed on the skate which is opposite to the direction the skater intends to turn.
2. The head, shoulders and arms rotate in the same direction as the turn. The free leg is positioned toward the outside, and the skate blade is placed at a 180-degree angle from the second skate, away from the skater and the second skate.
3. Weight is now shifted to the leg that has just turned. Then the other leg turns and is positioned parallel to the first leg. Using this technique, the skater can skate backward.

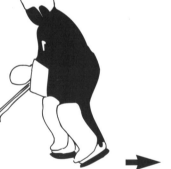

---

* This technique should be practiced from the right side and from the left side.

Backward start

1. The goalie is standing. The body's weight is shifted to the push skate, which rotates toward the inside so that the blade is at a 90-degree angle in relation to the desired direction.
2. The skater pushes strongly from the hip and knee, first toward the front, then toward the side, drawing the letter C on the rink surface.
3. The body's weight is then shifted to the other leg, which starts a new push.

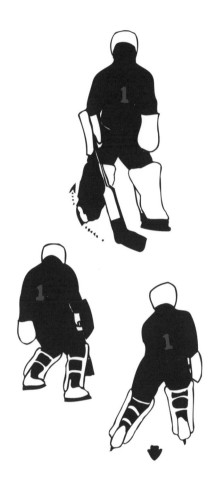

Backward skating

1. The goalie is in a sitting position, knees bent, torso slightly bent forward.
2. The body's weight is shifted to the push skate. A strong push from the hip and knee moves the goalie forward and sideways.
3. During the push, the skate draws the letter C on the rink surface; the body's weight is shifted to the other leg.
4. The same move is done alternately with each leg, drawing two elongated S shapes on the ice.

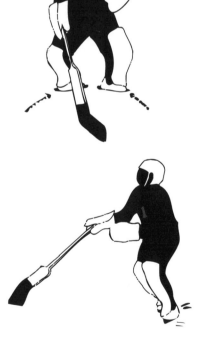

Backward stop (one skate)*

1. The body is bent forward and the front leg is deeply flexed.
2. The back skate is turned perpendicular to the skater's direction, and the body's weight is almost entirely on the back leg.
3. After absorbing the shock produced by the stop by bending the knee of the back leg, the goalie can either return to a standing or basic position or begin a forward or backward start.

Backward stop (two skates)

1. The body is bent far forward. Skates turn to the outside, forming an arc that ends where the heels almost touch.
2. During the stop, the body's weight is on the end of the skate blades.
3. When the stop is complete, blades are very close together and the goalie can either return to a stading or basic position or begin a forward or backward start.

---

* This technique should be practiced using the right leg and the left leg.

Backward crossover*

1. The head, body and shoulders are turned toward the inside of the crease and the torso is bent slightly forward.
2. The outside skate pushes. Meanwhile, the body's weight is shifted to the inside leg, which begins a new push.
3. During the inside leg's push, the outside leg is brought back toward the inside, moving in front of the push skate.
4. When the push ends, the inside skate is repositioned toward the center of the crease, moving behind the outside skate.

Pivot (from backward to forward skating)*

1. By slightly straightening the knees and body and bringing skates closer together, the body's weight is placed on the skate opposite the direction the skater intends to turn in.
2. The head, shoulders and arms rotate in the same direction as the turn. The free leg is brought up and directed toward the outside, in the desired direction.
3. When the skate touches the ice, the other leg is used to produce a strong push. Now the skater can skate forward.

31

This technique should be practiced using the right leg and the left leg.

CHAPTER 2

BASIC
TECHNIQUES

SUMMARY

1. Explain why it is important for a goalie to learn basic techniques as a beginner.

2. Describe each of the basic techniques a beginner goalie needs.

3. Outline a few exercises to develop each of the basic techniques described earlier.

4. Briefly describe three theoretical concepts that the beginner goalie should master.

	1	2	3	4
Period	Preseason	Season	Playoffs	Postseason
Month	J A	S O N D J F	M A	M J
A On-ice training		2 — Basic techniques		
B Off-ice training				

The difference between a goalie and any other hockey player is that, apart from skating techniques, almost all the other basic techniques he needs to learn are totally different from those that his teammates learns.

Until a goalie can stop worrying about technique, he will be unable to give 100% of his concentration to the game and the need to take split-second decisions.

It's very unfortunate to see beginner goalies playing on Bantam (13–14 years old) or Midget (15–16 years old) teams who still have a hard time with moves required in basic goaltending positions. In these categories the game is very fast, and the goalie needs total command of basic techniques to be effective in the net.

Ideally, such techniques should be learned in the first stage of the goalie's development (9 to 12 years old).

At the beginner's stage games aren't remarkably fast. The young goalie has an extraordinary ability to learn, and technical defects have not become a second nature to him.

The following pages focus on the various basic techniques needed for the proper development of a beginner goalie.

The basic standing position

1. Skates are more than one shoulder-width apart. The opening between pads is wide.
2. Knees are slightly bent and close together. The goalie is almost in a sitting position.

3. The torso is bent slightly forward and the head is held high so that the goalie can keep a close watch on the game.

4. Gloves are positioned at knee height but in front of the body to keep them within the goalie's field of vision. Both elbows are slightly bent and held toward the front.*
5. The stick is positioned 12 to 18 inches (30 to 45 cm) away from the goalie, at an angle to direct the puck into the corners of the rink.
6. The body's weight is placed squarely on the front of the foot. The entire length of the skate blade is in contact with the rink surface. On the other hand, the heel of the foot is slightly raised inside the skate.
7. The stick is held above the paddle (widened portion of the goal stick). The index finger is positioned on the widest part of the stick, while the other fingers are positioned around the shaft. This grasp gives better control of the stick during saves or one-handed passes.

Exercises to improve the basic standing position

The goalie skates as instructed by the coach, in the basic standing position or like a forward player.

---

* Positioning the gloves within the field of vision seems to improve the beginner goalie's coordination significantly, while also making it easier for him to use the catch glove effectively.

In the basic standing position, the goalie puts one knee on the ice and returns to the basic position as quickly as possible. Use each knee alternately.

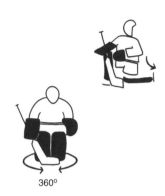

In the basic standing position, the goalie makes a 360-degree turn and returns to the basic position. He turns right and left.

360°

In the basic standing position, the goalie crouches when the coach brings the stick close to his head, and then jumps to let the stick move pass his skates. After each movement, the goalie quickly comes back to the basic standing position.

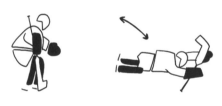

In the basic standing position, the goalie lies on his stomach and returns to his original position as quickly as possible.

In the basic standing position, the goalie move to the right and to the left, crossing one leg over the other. The rest of his body remains in the basic position.

In the basic standing position, with one of his gloves the goalie touches the rink surface behind him and then returns to the basic position. He uses each glove alternately.

The goalie moves forward in the basic standing position. Each time he encounters a puck, he jumps over it and immediately returns to the basic standing position.

While the goalie is in the basic standing position, the coach or another goalie pushes him, trying to throw him off balance. After each push, the goalie must return to the basic standing position as quickly as possible.

The basic crouching position*

1. Skates are a bit more than one shoulder-width apart. The opening between pads is wide.
2. Knees are very bent and close together. The goalie is almost in a sitting position.
3. The torso is bent far forward and is almost horizontal. The head is kept high to maintain a close watch on the game.
4. Gloves are positioned at knee height, but slightly in front of the knees. Elbows are bent almost completely.
5. The stick, 12 to 18 inches (30 to 45 cm) in front of the skates, is at an angle to direct pucks into the corner of the rink.
6. The body's weight is almost on the toes.

---

* This technical move is used mainly when there is a large amount of traffic in front of the net or against a deking forward player. In addition to adopting a crouching position, the goalie must attempt to keep his eye on the puck in the types of situations described here.

Exercises to improve the basic crouching position

The goalie skates as instructed by the coach, in the basic standing position, crouching or positioned like a forward player.

In the basic crouching position, the goalie follows puck movements by looking through the coach's legs.

In the basic crouching position, the goalie follows the movement of the puck.

The same exercise, but with a player or another goalie screening the puck.

In the basic crouching position, the goalie fields shots from different directions and distances.

The same exercise, but with a player or another goalie screening the puck.

The same exercise, but with two players screening the puck.

The basic kneeling position

1. Pads are as far apart as possible and touching the rink surface along their entire length.
2. The torso is straight and the goalie's bottom is positioned high to cover as much space as possible in the top portion of the net. The head is kept high to follow the game.
3. Gloves are positioned on each side of the body.
4. Held at an angle to direct pucks into the corner of the rink, the stick is positioned directly in front of the opening between the goalie's the legs.
5. The body's weight is placed on the knees.

Note that many goalies do not have the hip and knee flexibility to execute this technical move perfectly.

A different technical move is as effective when shots are low.

1. Simply stretch out the pad on the side where the puck is shot.
2. The other pad stays positioned toward the back.
3. For other parts of the body, this technical move is identical to the basic kneeling position.

Exercises to improve the basic kneeling position

The goalie goes from the basic standing position to the basic kneeling position:
 a) with both pads spread to the side;
 b) with only one pad spread to the side.

a   b

The goalie goes from the basic standing position to a facedown position and back to the basic kneeling position:
 a) with both pads spread to the side;
 b) with only one pad spread to the side.

The goalie goes from the basic crouching position to the basic kneeling position:
 a) with both pads spread to the side;
 b) with only one pad spread to the side.

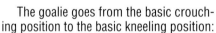

a   b

The goalie is in the basic kneeling position. Pads are positioned toward the back. On the coach's instructions, the goalie: (a) spreads the right pad to the side; (b) spreads the left pad to the side; (c) or spreads both pads to the side.

The goalie is in the basic kneeling position. Pads are positioned toward the back. Depending on the puck's direction, the goalie spreads his left or right pad to the side.

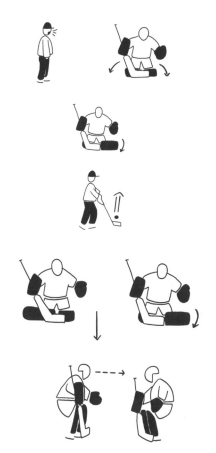

The goalie is in the basic kneeling position. Pads are positioned toward the back. He moves forward by alternately moving his pads to the side.

Two goalies are face to face. The goalie designated by the coach adopts the basic standing, crouching or kneeling position, with one or two pads positioned to the side. The other goalie must react appropriately by imitating the same move.

Forward movement in the basic standing position*

1. The goalie is in the basic standing position.
2. The goalie does an outside turn on the push skate (close to 90 degrees from the desired direction).
3. Weight is shifted to the push skate and a strong extension toward the back is produced by the hip and knee of the push leg. The push produces a forward movement.

43

---

* This type of move is used to follow the puck.

4. Throughout the movement, only the push leg should change places. The rest of the body remains in the basic position, which means that the goalie is constantly ready to field a shot.
5. To stop, the goalie turns the other leg's skate to place it at a 90-degree angle in relation to the direction of his movement. The body's weight is placed on the front of the skate blade. The goalie must be careful to keep his body pointed toward the puck. As soon as the puck is stopped, he must return immediately to his initial basic position.

Backward movement in the basic standing position

1. The goalie is in the basic standing position.
2. The goalie does an inside turn on the push skate (at close to a 90-degree angle from the desired direction).
3. Weight is shifted to the push skate and a strong extension toward the front and the side is produced by the hip and knee, drawing a C on the rink surface.
4. As soon as the push is completed, the goalie returns to his original position to begin a backward slide.
5. Throughout the movement, only the push leg should change places. The rest of the body remains in the basic position, which means that the goalie is constantly ready to field a shot.
6. To stop, the goalie turns only one skate, placing it at a 90-degree angle in relation to the direction of his turn.

7. The goalie must be careful to keep his body pointed toward the puck. As soon as the puck is stopped, he must return immediately to his initial basic position.

Exercises to develop forward and backward movement in the basic standing position

In the basic standing position, at a signal from the coach, the goalie moves quickly toward the front and returns to his initial position.

Repeat for backward movement.

Two goalies are face to face at a distance of 6 feet (1.8 m).

The goalie with the puck advances to pass it to his partner, who backs away.

When the second goalie has picked up the pass, he brakes and advances, while his partner backs away.

In the basic standing position, the goalie makes a variety of moves in relation to his net.

45

In the basic standing position, the goalie advances and clears a puck placed in front of his goal. Then he backs into his goal and clears another puck.

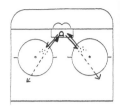

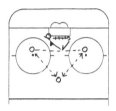 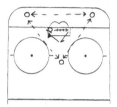 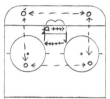 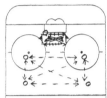

In the basic standing position, the goalie moves to follow the puck.

In the basic standing position, the goalie moves to follow the puck, then fields a shot.

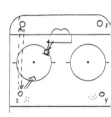

Player 2 passes to 1, who passes back to 2, who shoots. Then 4 passes to 3, who passes back to 4, who shoots.

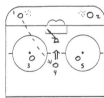

Player 1 passes to 3, 4 or 5, who shoots on the goal. Then Player 2 passes to 3, 4 or 5.

Player 1 passes to 2, who passes to 3, who shoots on the goal.

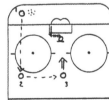

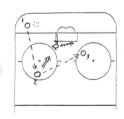

Player 1 passes to 2, who has the choice of shooting on the goal or passing to 3.

Movement in the basic standing position, skates parallel*

1. If the movement is toward the right side, the goalie must begin by shifting his weight to the inside edge of the left skate blade.
2. Once his weight has been shifted, a strong extension of the left leg moves the goalie to the right. The right skate is parallel to the left skate and the blade should be flat on the ice to reduce friction to a minimum if the movement is short.
3. When the movement is prolonged, the goalie can open the right skate to make movement easier.
4. The rest of the body remains in the basic position throughout the movement, to ensure that the goalie is constantly prepared to field a shot.
5. An identical but inverse process is used to move from left to right.

Exercises to improve movement in the basic standing position, skates parallel

The goalie is in the basic standing position. For a movement to the right, the goalie spreads his left leg to the right and brings his left leg back to the center.

The goalie is in the basic standing position. For a movement to the right, the goalie pushes strongly with the left leg and lets his right skate glide on the ice.

47

---

* This technical movement is used to follow the puck or to go from one goal post to the other.

In the basic standing position, the goalie follows the coach's instructions.

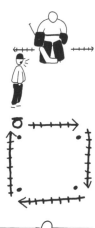

In a basic standing position, the goalie moves around four pucks placed to form a 6 feet (1.8 m) square.

In the basic standing position, the goalie move from one goal post to the other.

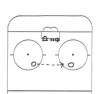

Two goalies stand face to face. The goalie designated by the coach positions himself to the left or to the right, in the basic standing position. His partner imitates his movements.

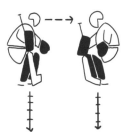

In the basic standing position, the goalie follows the pass and moves with his skates in a parallel position.

In the basic standing position, the goalie fields a pass from Player 1. Player 1 then passes to Player 2, who shoots on the goal.

In the basic standing position, the goalie fields a pass from Player 1, who approaches him. Immediately after, Player 2, who is immobile, shoots on the goal.

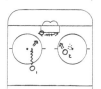

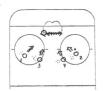

In the basic standing position, the goalie fields passes from players positioned in a predetermined order.

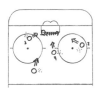

In the basic standing position, the goalie fields passes from players positioned in a different predetermined order.

Immobilizing the puck

1. The goalie is in the basic standing position.
2. When the puck is near the goalie or when he has just allowed a rebound, he can kneel down on both knees.
3. To prevent an opponent from robbing the puck, he places his catch glove and stick or his blocker on the puck.
4. When the goalie is in the basic kneeling position, the move is identical.
5. If the goalie is forced to dive facedown to immobilize the puck, he should attempt the same move, but should be very careful not to push the puck forward or cause it to slide under him.
6. Regardless of the position, the goalie should keep his head high and his eyes on rival players, his gloves and the puck.

Exercises to develop the technique of immobilizing the puck

The goalie is in the basic standing position. Several pucks are shot toward him.

On the coach's instructions, the goalie immobilizes one of the pucks.

49

The coach shoots throws toward the goalie. As soon as a puck touches the rink surface, the goalie immobilizes it.

In the basic standing position, the goalie juggles a puck. As soon as the puck hits the rink surface, he immobilizes it.

The coach handles the puck very close to the goalie. When the goalie thinks he sees an opportunity, he immobilizes the puck.

In the basic standing position, the goalie blocks, then immobilizes, pucks shot on his goal.

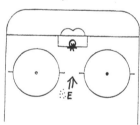

In the basic kneeling position, the goalie blocks, then immobilizes, pucks shot on his goal.

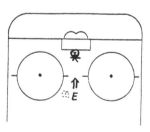

Note that, for each of these exercises, the goalie can immobilize the puck:
— on both knees on the ice;
— facedown on the ice.

The kneeling-standing movement

1. The goalie is in the basic kneeling position.
2. He straightens one leg and places the skate blade on the ice.
3. He immediately adopts the basic standing position. Throughout the movement, his gloves, stick and head must be immobile. Only his legs should move.
4. Note that the goalie should practice this move with the right leg and the left leg.

Exercises to develop the kneeling-standing movement

In the basic kneeling position, the goalie straightens his left leg and returns to the basic standing position. He practices the same move using the right leg.

The goalie is facedown. He moves onto his knees and then returns to the basic standing position.

In the basic kneeling position, the goalie throws a ball into the air. He returns to the basic standing position to catch it.

In the basic standing position, the goalie crouches to adopt the basic kneeling position, then returns to his original position.

In the basic standing position, the goalie move forward, stops, adopts a basic kneeling position, gets up and moves backward.

In the basic standing position, the goalie moves to the right, with skates parallel, adopts a basic kneeling position, gets up and moves to the left.

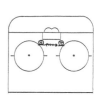

In the basic standing position, the goalie fields a high shot, then a low shot that he blocks with his pads, and so on.

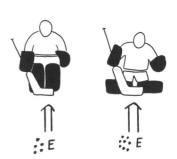

Harpooning a corner shot

1. The goalie is adjacent to a goal post, leaning on it hard with his skate and pad.
2. The goalie's body is pointed toward the front of the net with only his head turned to the back. Knees are bent and skates are parallel for quick movement forward or to the opposite goal post.
3. The stick is positioned on the side of the net, as close as possible to the goal line.
4. The goalie must be ready to deflect the puck or to stop it, by flexing or extending his stick-arm.
5. The catch glove is outside the net and opened wide to catch high shots.
6. If the puck is shot from the opposite side of the net, the goalie moves quickly to the other goal post and adopts the same position.

Exercises to develop the technique for harpooning a corner shot

Positioned close to the goal post, the goalie harpoons the puck shot on his goal. The goalie can:
— harpoon and return the puck behind the net;
— harpoon and immobilize the puck.

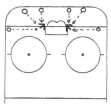

Positioned close to the goal post, the goalie harpoons pucks shot on his goal by players on the move.

The goalie can:
— harpoon and return the puck behind the net;
— harpoon and immobilize the puck.

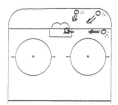

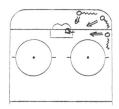

Positioned close to the goal post, the goalie harpoons pucks shot on his goal. If the goalie fails to harpoon the puck, the player positioned in front of the net can shoot it.

Positioned close to the goal post, the goalie watches the movements of Player 1, who attempts to pass to Player 2 through the goal crease.

Watching the puck behind the net

1. In the basic standing position, the goalie is close to the goal line.
2. His knees are bent more slightly than usual to let him move quickly, depending on the direction taken by opponents.
3. Only his head is turned in the direction of the puck. If the puck is on the right of the center of the crossbar, the goalie turns his head to the right and moves in the same direction. If the puck is on the left of the center of the crossbar, the goalie turns his head to the left and moves in the same direction.
4. When a player tries to pass the puck or moves to the front of the net, the goalie adopts the same position as he does to harpoon a corner shot (see preceding basic technique).

When a goalie is watching a puck behind his net, the following two errors are very common.

Exercises to develop the technique for watching a puck behind the net

The goalie must observe and move based on the player skating with the puck behind his net.

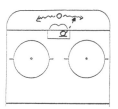

The goalie must observe and move based on how the puck moves.

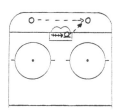

The goalie must observe and move based on how the puck moves.

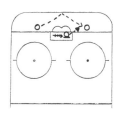

Moving out behind the net

1. In the basic standing position, the goalie watches the player in a position to shoot.
2. When the puck is cleared along the boards, the goalie moves to face the play, opens the skate closest to the boards and pushes with the opposite leg.
3. When he is close to the boards, the goalie returns to the basic standing position and positions his stick along the boards to stop the puck.
4. When the puck is stopped, the goalie returns to his net as quickly as possible, opening the skate closest to the net and pushing with the opposite leg.
5. Once he has returned to his net on the same side as he came out, the goalie adopts a position identical to the one used for harpooning a corner shot.

Right exit

Left exit

Exercises to develop the technique for moving out behind the net

In the basic standing position, the goalie is in the corner of his goal. He moves to the right of the boards, touches them with his stick and returns to his net immediately.

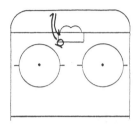

In the basic standing position, the goalie is in the corner of his goal.

When the coach shoots a puck along the boards, the goalie comes out to stop it.

If the goalie anticipates the play, the coach can shoot directly at the net.

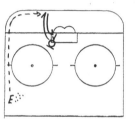

In the basic standing position, the goalie is in the corner of his goal.

When the coach shoots a puck along the boards, the goalie comes out to stop it and returns the puck in the same direction.

In the basic standing position, the goalie is in the corner of his goal.

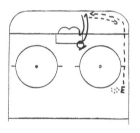

When the coach shoots a puck along the boards, the goalie comes out to stop it and passes it to a player skating at center ice.

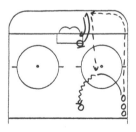

Two-handed puck handling

1. The goalie skates in the standing position.
2. He positions his blocker on the end of the stick and his catch glove just above the paddle (widened portion of the goal stick).
3. Note that arms and shoulders should be relaxed and elbows positioned away from the body.
4. The goalie pushes the puck to one side. Then the blade of the stick quickly passes over the puck to stop it. The puck is then pushed in the opposite direction and each of the previous steps is repeated.
5. The side dribble (the puck is dribbled in the same direction as the goalie is moving) usually holds the most advantages for goalies, since it is relatively easy to learn and the puck is easy to shoot.

Exercises to develop the technique for two-handed puck handling

The goalie handles the puck using two hands, skating forward and backward.

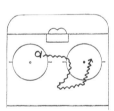

Standing still in the basic standing position, the goalie handles a medicine ball, using both hands.

One goalie handles the puck inside the icing circle. His partner skates after him to rob the puck.

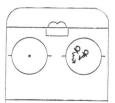

The goalie handles the puck through a course set out using cones. The goalie handles the puck, skating forward and backward.

Backhand pass using one hand

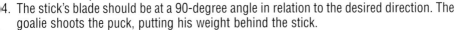
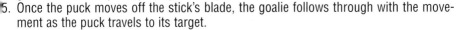

1. The goalie is in a position identical to that used to stop a puck shot from behind the net. The puck is brought back to the right side (for a goalie who wears the blocker on his right hand), approximately at skate height.
2. The stick shaft is leaned against the goalie's back and the puck is touching the stick's blade.
3. The body's weight is shifted to the skate closest to the puck.
4. The stick's blade should be at a 90-degree angle in relation to the desired direction. The goalie shoots the puck, putting his weight behind the stick.
5. Once the puck moves off the stick's blade, the goalie follows through with the movement as the puck travels to its target.

Two-handed pass from the right*

1. The goalie is in a position identical to that used for two-handed handling. The puck is brought back to the side, while still in contact with the stick's blade, which is slightly bent over the puck.
2. The body's weight is on the skate which is on the same side as the puck. The goalie shoots the puck toward its target, putting his weight behind the stick. Weight is shifted from the back leg to the front leg.
3. The stick's blade should be at a 90-degree angle in relation to the desired direction. Once the puck moves off the stick's blade, the goalie follows through with the movement as the puck travels to its target. Elbows should be held away from the body.

59

---

* Shooting is not an issue for beginner goalies since most of them do not have the muscle power for this kind of technical move. They should limit themselves to handling and passing the puck as described here.

Exercises to develop one-handed and two-handed passing

The goalie must direct the puck between cones positioned at different locations on the rink surface.

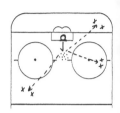

Two goalies are face to face. When the goalie with the puck moves forward with the puck, his partner backs away. When the pass is completed, the goalie with the puck advances and his partner backs away.

In the basic standing position, the goalie fields a shot. After stopping it, he passes the puck to the coach.

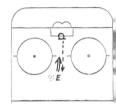

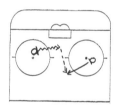

A goalie skates while handling the puck, and passes it to his partner.

The goalie moves forward, takes a puck and passes it to his coach, who can be positioned at various locations. When the pass is completed, the goalie returns to his net.

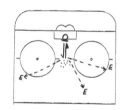

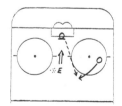

In the basic standing position, the goalie fields a shot. After stopping the puck he passes it to a player, positioned at various locations.

Note that, for each of these exercises, the goalie can pass the puck using one hand or two hands.

Techniques for stopping the puck*

Regardless of his age or the caliber of his team, the goalie must be prepared to field the following types of shots:
A. low shots;
B. shots of average height;
C. high shots.

In addition, shots can be directed:
A. to the right of the net;
B. to the center of the net;
C. to the left of the net.
The goalie's job is:

A. to control the puck (for example, with his catch glove);
B. to direct the puck (for example, with his stick);
C. or to absorb the puck (for example, with his torso).

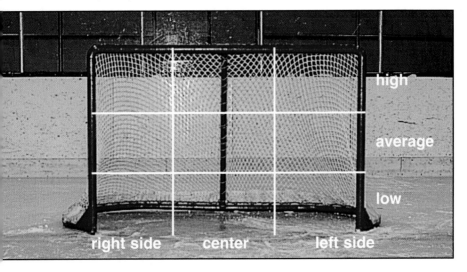

Therefore, a net can be divided into nine specific zones.
The order (right side, left side) corresponds to the goalie's position in front of the net.
For each zone, there are one or several techniques to stop the puck, with one or more corresponding pieces of equipment.

---

* When practicing stopping techniques, it is a good idea to vary the frequency and angle of shots, as well as the type of shot and its strength.

Techniques for stopping the puck on low shots

A Stick save — Characteristics:
height: low shot
direction: center of goal
task: to clear the puck

1. The goalie is in the basic standing position. He moves his stick in semicircles in front of him, depending on whether the puck is to his right or to his left.

2. He must be very careful to make sure that the entire length of his stick blade is in contact with the rink surface. To do so, he must keep his knees bent.

3. The goalie sends the puck to the corner of the rink.
4. He must keep his eye on the puck until it comes into contact with his stick.

Exercises to develop the stick-save technique

In the basic standing position, as the coach brings his stick close to the goalie's, the goalie hits it with his own stick.

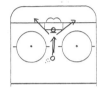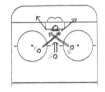

In the basic standing position, the goalie uses his stick to send the puck into the corners of the rink.
The goalie can be:
— in the basic standing position;
— in the basic kneeling position.

For high shots, the goalie should begin to learn stopping techniques with the kind of ball used to play street hockey. Later he can begin using felt pucks and, finally, he can practice with regular pucks.

3. Pad save — Characteristics:
   height: low shot
   direction: to the right or to the left of the net
   task: to clear the puck or absorb the shot

1. The goalie is in the basic kneeling position.
2. The goalie can send the puck to the corner of the rink by positioning his pad in the appropriate direction or he can absorb the shot by positioning his pad perpendicular to the direction taken by the puck. Then, using his gloves, the goalie must stop the puck immediately.
3. The goalie keeps his eye on the puck until it comes into contact with his pad.
4. The goalie can use the basic kneeling position, with both pads spread out to

each side; or he can position only one pad to the side, depending on the direction of the puck.

Exercises to develop the pad save technique (low shots)

In the basic kneeling position, the goalie uses his pads to send the puck to the corners of the rink.

The goalie can practice these shot exercises using the basic kneeling position as his starting position.

He can also start in the basic standing position, make the save in the basic kneeling position, and return to his initial position between shots.

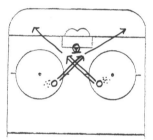

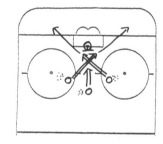

Techniques for stopping the puck on average height shots*

A. Catch glove save — Characteristics:
   height: average height shot
   direction: to the right or to the left, depending on which hand is the catch glove hand
   task: to control the puck

1. The goalie is in the basic standing position.
2. He must stay in the basic standing position, on balance, throughout the save.
3. The goalie must keep his eye on the puck until it is in his catch glove.
4. The skate on the same side as the catch glove is used to make a T-push. A push using the other skate sends the goalie in the proper direction to make a save with his catch glove.

Exercises to develop the catch-glove save technique (average-height shots)

In the basic standing position, the goalie throws a ball against the boards and catches it in one hand.

Two goalies face to face in the basic standing position throw a ball to each other.

Two goalies stand face to face and throw each other a puck, which they catch with their catch glove.

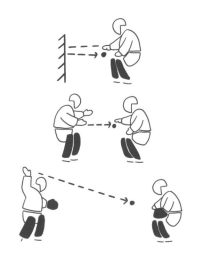

65

---

* Because they are too small to block the entire net opening, beginner goalies must make frequent use of the T-push technique when stopping shots.

In the basic standing position, the goalie makes a save with his catch glove. The goalie can make the save:
— in the basic standing position;
— using a T-push move.

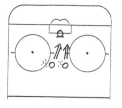

In the basic standing position, the goalie is positioned near a goal post. The forward player shoots the puck toward the opposite corner of the net. The goalie uses a T-push move to make a save with his catch glove.

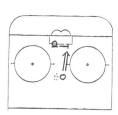

In the basic standing position, the goalie makes a save with his catch glove, then makes a one-handed or two-handed pass to a player positioned near the net.

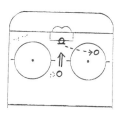

B. Blocker save — Characteristics:
   height: average-height shot
   direction: to the right or to the left, depending on which hand is the catch glove hand
   task: to clear the puck

1. The goalie is in the basic standing position.
2. He must stay in the basic standing position, on balance, throughout the save.
3. The goalie must keep his eye on the puck until it comes into contact with his blocker.

4. A flick of the wrist toward the corner of the rink sends the puck in that direction.
5. The skate on the same side as the blocker is used to make a T-push move. A push using the other skate sends the goalie in the proper direction to make a save with his blocker.
6. To control the puck, the goalie must trap it between his blocker and his catch glove when it comes into contact with the blocker.

Exercises to develop the blocker save technique (average-height shots)

In the basic standing position, the goalie juggles a puck by bouncing it on his blocker.

The goalie throws a puck into the air and catches it by trapping it between his blocker and his catch glove.

Two goalies stand face to face and throw each other a puck; they take turns deflecting it with their blocker.

Two goalies stand face to face and throw each other a puck; they take turns trapping it between their blocker and their catch glove.

In the basic standing position, the goalie makes a save with his blocker.
The goalie can make the save:
— in the basic standing position;
— using a T-push move.

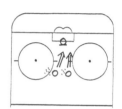

He can also:
— send the puck into the corner of the rink;
— trap the puck between his blocker and his catch glove;
— pass the puck to a player positioned near the net.

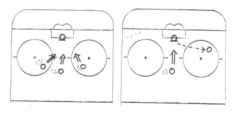

C. Upper body save — Characteristics:
height: average-height shots
direction: toward the center of the net
task: to absorb the shot

1. The goalie is in the basic kneeling position. He should not be sitting on his skates since he must cover as much space as possible toward the top of the net.
2. He must absorb the puck with his body, not hit it. As soon as the puck comes into contact with his body, the goalie must attempt to immobilize the puck, using one or both arms.

3. Alternatively, he can let the puck fall to the ice and immobilize it with his gloves.
4. The goalie must keep his eye on the puck until it is immobilized in his arms or his gloves.

Exercises to develop the upper-body save technique (average-height shots)

The coach tosses pucks at the goalie, who is in the basic kneeling position.

In the basic kneeling position, the goalie fields shots from another player, using felt balls.

In the basic kneeling position, the goalie fields pucks shot from close range.

In the basic standing position, the goalie advances toward Player 1. Player 1 passes to Player 2, who shoots on goal, with the puck at average height. The goalie moves and goes into the basic kneeling position to make the save.

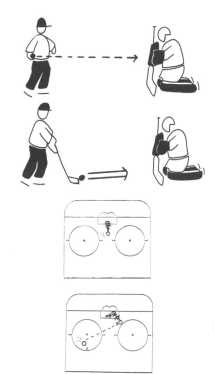

69

Techniques for stopping the puck on high shots

A. Catch glove save — Characteristics:
height: high shot
direction: to the right or to the left, depending on which hand is the catch-glove hand
task: to control the puck

1. The same move as the catch-glove save at average height, but with the catch glove positioned higher.
2. Instead of a half-butterfly stance, the goalie should use a T-push to move in the direction of the puck.

Exercises to develop the catch-glove save technique (high shots)*

The exercises designed to develop the catch-glove save technique for average-height shots can also be used for high shots.

---

* *Because they are too small to block the entire net opening, beginner goalies should remain standing to stop high shots into the corner of the net.*

B. Blocker save — Characteristics:
height: high shot
direction: to the right or to the left,
depending on which hand is the catch-
glove hand
task: to clear or control the puck

1. The same move as the blocker save at
average height, but with the blocker
positioned higher.
2. Instead of a half-butterfly stance, the
goalie should use a T-push to move in
the direction of the puck.
3. To control the puck, the goalie must
trap it between his blocker and his
catch glove when it comes into contact
with his blocker.

Exercises to develop the blocker save technique (high shots)*

The exercises designed to develop the blocker save technique for average-height shots
can also be used for high shots.

---

* Because they are too small to block the entire net opening, beginner goalies should remain standing to stop high shots
into the corner of the net.

C. Upper-body save — Characteristics:
height: high shot
direction: center of the net
task: to absorb and control the puck

1. The same move as the upper-body save for average-height shots.
2. The goalie must bring both arms close to his body so that there is no opening between his torso and his arms.
3. For this type of save, using one or both arms the goalie must trap the puck against his stomach, preventing the puck from falling to the ice.

Exercises to develop the upper-body save technique (high shots)

The exercises designed to develop the upper-body save technique for average-height shots can also be used for high shots.

Theoretical concepts

Theoretically, the beginner goalie should be able to understand and apply the following concepts fairly well:
A — movement
B — positioning
C — space coverage

Although most training related to these three concepts should be done mainly when goalies have reached the intermediate stage (13 to 16 years old), it is vital to begin the learning process when goalies are 9 to 12 years old.

This is why each of the three concepts is explained briefly, with skating and basic techniques used as the focus of on-ice training.

A — Movement

This principle requires good skating ability on the part of the goalie. Every time there is a pass from the defense zone, the goalie must use a push movement to follow the puck as it is passed from one player to another.

Exercises to develop the movement concept

(Review the skating and movement exercises outlined in Chapter 1.)

B — Positioning

After the pass, when the puck is on the opponent's stick, the goalie must stop and position himself directly in front of the puck (he must not position himself in front of the player). He should have one skate on each side of an imaginary line that links the center of the net to the puck.

wrong position   wrong position

Exercises to develop the positioning concept

The coach ties a rope to the crossbar of the net. He stretches the rope over pucks that are spread out at different angles.

The goalie must move about while keeping one skate on each side of the rope.

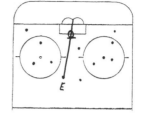

In the basic standing position, the goalie has one foot on each side of the rope.

Another goalie observes shot angles by positioning himself at eye level with the puck.

The goalie in the net can position his two feet to the right or to the left of the rope to help his partner visualize shot angles as clearly as possible.

The coach ties one end of a rope to the crossbar of the net and the other to his stick blade.

He moves to the left and to the right. The goalie must keep one skate on each side of the rope.

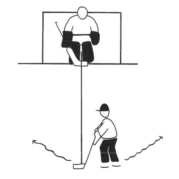

In the basic standing position, the goalie positions himself facing the puck.

The coach positions himself behind the puck and makes corrections as needed.

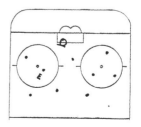

75

C — Space coverage

When the beginner goalie is aware of the concepts of movement and positioning, it is fairly simple to introduce the concept of covering space.

The deeper a goalie stays in his goal, the more openings he leaves for forward players.

On the other hand, the more a goalie advances in the forward player's direction, the more space he covers.

Given the fact that open space is at its maximum in front of the net, the goalie should advance over a short distance to cover the openings available to a player positioned in front of the net.

For shots from a sharper angle, the goalie need not advance as far out of the net because there is a smaller amount of open space.

Usually, the goalie's moves toward the puck should look something like a semicircle that is elongated toward the front.

This type of movement toward the puck provides maximum space coverage, regardless of which direction the puck is shot from.

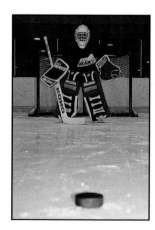

Of course, movement is based on specific criteria:
— the goalie's skating ability (the better the skater, the further he can go out of his goal);
— the certainty that a player will shoot on the net (when the goalie is sure that the puck will be shot, he can advance a little further to cover the maximum amount of space). It is very important to understand that the goalie must move toward the puck before it is shot toward the net. As soon as the puck is shot, the goalie must stand still for maximum stability and balance;
— the possibility that another play will be made at the last minute (on a 2 against 1 or 3 against 1 offense, the goalie should not advance too far toward the skater who has possession of the puck).

Generally, the goalie's heels move along an imaginary line that runs along the semicircle described previously.

From this position, the goalie can begin forward and backward movements, or movements to the right or to the left.*

Exercises to develop the space coverage concept

The goalie is in the basic standing position, on the goal line, facing the puck.

A second goalie observes the space coverage by positioning himself at eye level with the puck.

The goalie in the net slowly advances toward the puck.

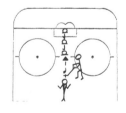

The same exercise, but with the puck positioned toward the right or toward the left of the net.

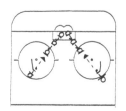

---

* It is false to think that a beginner goalie can cover a great deal of space because of:
— the size of the net (the same size as nets used in the NHL);
— the goalie's height (between 3.5 and 4.5 feet/1.06 and 1.37 m on average).

The coach ties the two ends of a rope to each of the net's vertical posts and stretches the rope into a triangle shape.

In the basic standing position, the goalie advances toward the puck, realizing that there is less and less space between his body and the ropes.

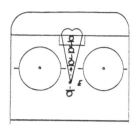

A second goalie observes the space coverage by positioning himself at eye level with the puck.

The coach positions himself to shoot the puck.

The goalie covers space while following the puck's position. The coach can also shoot the puck toward the net.

The second goalie observes by positioning himself at eye level with the puck.

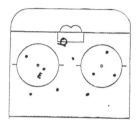

The goalie fields shots from very wide and very sharp angles. The goalie must realize that he does not need to advance as far out for shots from sharp angles.

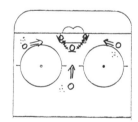

CHAPTER 3

ON-ICE EVALUATION
OF GOALIES

Summary

1. Describe the objectives of evaluating beginner goalies.
2. Outline a method for applying tests before, during and after evaluation.
3. Outline selected tests and the application procedures required for each test.
4. Describe briefly a few of the qualities to look for when selecting beginner goalies.

	1	2	3	4
Period	Preseason	Season	Playoffs	Postseason
Month	J A	S O N D J F	M A	M J
A On-ice training		3 — On-ice evaluation ⊢—⁄ ⊢—⁄ ⊢—⁄		
B Off-ice training				

E valuating goalies is a very important part of a coach's job. Unfortunately, very little material exists on the subject, and very often the coach must rely on his own instincts when selecting his goalies and evaluating their progress during the hockey season.

This chapter outlines tests selected on the basis of:

1. their effectiveness in evaluating the qualities required of a beginner goalie;
2. their ease of use;
3. the amount of material they require.

Although they cannot guarantee absolute success in evaluating your goalies, they can at least provide a good comparison scale.

The objective of evaluating goalies both on and off the ice are the following:

1. To determine the level of quality the goalies have achieved, based on physical and technical objectives (selection).
2. To diagnose the goalies' strengths and weaknesses (training plan).
3. To observe improvements in goalies (progress).

How to apply the tests

When applying evaluation tests, it is very important to be aware of certain information regarding how to proceed.

In addition, it is very important that the instructions for each test be repeated in the same way for each participant, every time the test is used.

Before applying the tests

1. Thorough knowledge of the tests

The coach must be familiar with the procedures for applying the tests he chooses. In addition, goalies must be given the chance to do the tests a few times. Inexperience may prevent a goalie from reaching his best performance levels during testing.

2. Availability of material, ice and time

Preparing the material and ice surface needed for the tests ahead of time can make the testing process easier and can eliminate the time otherwise allocated to these particular tasks at the time of the test.

The entire series of tests should not be applied on the same day. A more reasonable approach would be to apply them over two or three training sessions.

During the tests

1. Warm-up time

To reach optimal performance levels, just as he would before a game, the goalie needs time to warm up.

2. Test demonstrations and explanations

Before beginning a test, is important to provide a demonstration and clear explanations.

3. Motivation

Motivation is very important when someone's physical skills are being tested. The coach should make sure that each goalie is given the same level of encouragement.

After applying the tests

1. Interpreting results

When the tests are completed, the coach must interpret the results. This will enable him to identify each goalie's strengths and weaknesses to begin his final selection, plan his training sessions, or evaluate the progress made by each of his goalies.

On-ice tests*

On-ice evaluation tests are used to measure the following:

A — Agility on the ice

1. Test objective:
To measure the beginner goalie's agility on the ice.

2. Material required:
— 1 pencil
— 1 whistle
— 1 result sheet
— 1 stopwatch

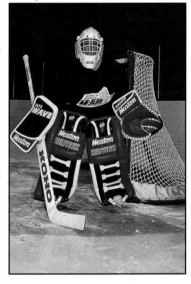

3. Goalie's clothing:
The goalie wears his full equipment and keeps his stick throughout the test.

---

* These tests have not undergone the experimental steps needed for their final validation.

4. Procedure:
— The goalie is in the basic position.
— On a signal, the goalie lies facedown on the ice. He quickly returns to the standing position, then lies on his back, then quickly stands again. This sequence is one full cycle. The goalie must run through the cycle correctly five times.
— The coach stops the stopwatch when the goalie correctly returns to his initial basic position.
— The time is recorded to the nearest second.
— If the goalie stops, the test is done over again. On the second attempt, the stopwatch continues to run.

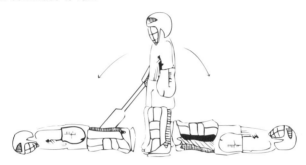

B — Puck-handling ability

1. Test objective:
To measure the beginner goalie's puck-handling ability.

2. Material required:
— 1 pencil
— 1 result or compilation sheet
— 1 stopwatch
— 1 puck
— 1 whistle

3. Goalie's clothing: See Test A.

4. Procedure:
— The goalie is in the basic position in his goal. His stick and his skates should be inside the goal line.
— On a signal, the goalie starts out quickly and positions his stick on the puck placed between the two lines of the face-off circle. He skates around the circle while handling the puck, moves behind and around the net, and skates toward the second face-off circle. When both his skates are inside the second face-off circle, he shoots the puck toward the blue line, brakes, and skates backwards to the net, where he returns to the basic position.
— The coach stops the stopwatch when the goalie correctly returns to his final basic position.
— Time is recorded to the nearest second.
— If the goalie falls or loses control of the puck, the test is done over again. On the second attempt, the stopwatch continues to run.

Forward movement   ——→

Backward movement   ◄———

Puck handling   ∿∿∿»

Pass   - - - -»

Puck   •

Stop   ∿|

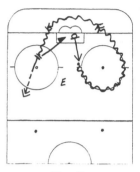

Test B

C — Speed of parallel movements

1. Test objective:
To measure the speed of parallel movements.

2. Material required:
— 1 pencil
— 1 compilation sheet
— 1 stopwatch
— 1 whistle

3. Goalie's clothing: See Test A.

4. Procedure:
— The goalie is in the basic position on the goal line. One of his skates must rest against one of the two goal posts.
— On a signal, in the basic position the goalie moves toward the opposite goal post. When he reaches the other side of the net, he must rest his skate on the goal post and then return in the opposite direction to touch the first goal post again. This sequence is one full cycle.
— The coach stops the stopwatch when the goalie has run through five complete cycles.
— Time is recorded to the nearest second.
— If the goalie falls or stops, the test is done over again. On the second attempt, the stopwatch continues to run.

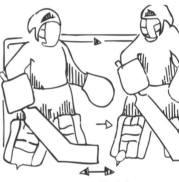

Test C

D — Speed of forward and backward skating

1. Test objective:
To measure the speed of forward and backward skating in the basic position.

2. Material required:
— 1 pencil
— 1 whistle
— 1 result sheet
— 1 stopwatch
— 1 tape measure
— 5 pucks

3. Goalie's clothing: See Test A.

4. Procedure:
—The goalie is in the basic position in the goal. His skates and stick must be inside the goal line.
—On a signal, in the basic position the goalie moves quickly toward a puck, touching it with his skate. Note that the goalie must keep his hand on the stick's shaft and must not harpoon the puck.
—In the basic position, he skates backward into the goal. When his skates and stick are inside the crease, the goalie can begin again, skating forward to touch another puck. The same sequence is repeated using five different pucks.
—The entire trajectory should be covered in the basic position.
—The coach stops the stopwatch when the goalie correctly returns to the basic position in the goal.
—Time is recorded to the nearest second.
—If the goalie falls, the test is done over again. On the second attempt, the stopwatch continues to run.

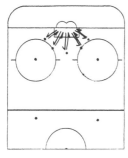

Test D

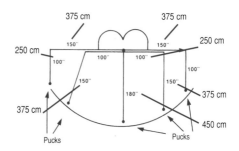

Measurements for the positioning of the pucks used in Test D.

E — Puck-stopping ability

1. Test objective:
To measure the beginner goalie's puck stopping ability.

2. Material required:
— 1 pencil
— 1 observation sheet
— 20 pucks

3. Goalie's clothing: See Test A.

4. Procedure:
—The goalie is in the basic position, just outside the goal (heels close to the goal line).
—The assistant coach is positioned in the enclave, approximately 20 to 30 feet (6 to 9 m) behind the face-off lines.
—The puck is shot toward the net at a specific and predetermined height.

The pace should allow the goalie enough time to return to the basic position between shots.

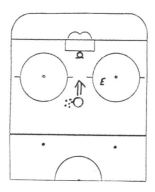

— Each goalie should field:
  a) 15 low shots, which he must stop with his stick or his pads (five pucks to the left, five to the center, five to the right);
  b) 15 average height shots, which he must stop with his pads, his body, his blocker or his catch glove (five pucks to the center, five to the left, five to the right);
  c) 15 high shots, which he must stop with his body, his catch glove or his blocker (five pucks to the center, five to the left, five to the right).

— The coach must only take note of shots that are made at the proper height, at the proper time (for example, a high shot in the low-shot sequence is not noted).
— The coach notes the number of shots stopped by each goalie, at each height. In addition, he observes the style, speed of movement, balance and courage shown by each goalie.

Objective and subjective at the same time, this test can provide very valuable information during your final selection process.

Qualities to observe

Because of a lack of time or assistance, it is not always possible to have all young goalies take the on-ice and off-ice evaluation tests.

When such a situation occurs (or to improve the quality of tests), the coach should observe the following points:

A) Does the goalie move quickly?

It is very important for a goalie to move quickly, since his work is often based on speed. Make sure your goalie is quick and energetic.

B) Is the goalie competitive?

It is crucial that your goalie feel at ease and aggressive during sports competitions; if not, at times he will not be able to withstand the tension and pressure they can involve.

C) Does the goalie take advice willingly?

A goalie who refuses to follow advice will not show quick progress and will remain at the same level of skill.
It should be easy to choose between a receptive goalie and an unreceptive goalie.

D) Does the goalie show courage?

A goalie absolutely needs to show courage if he wants to succeed. In fact, if each time he faces a shot he raises his shoulders, turns his head or backs deep into his goal, his basic position will never be adequate and he will never be happy tending goal.

E) Is the goalie a hard worker?

A goalie who has this particular quality will work tirelessly to improve the basic moves he needs and to correct the defects his coach points out to him.
Furthermore, a hardworking goalie shows beyond any doubt that he has discipline and perseverance, both of which are very important.

F) Is the goalie a good skater?

Since skating is the most important technical aspect of hockey, the goalie must have a fairly good command of skating techniques to succeed.
In addition, a good skater who likes to tend goal will almost always be a very good goalie.

G) Does the goalie have good coordination?

Hand–eye coordination and foot–eye coordination are vital for trapping or stopping some shots directed toward the goalie.
If the goalie does not show any degree of ease or precision in catching balls thrown to him or kicked toward him, you can almost be sure that goaltending is not a job he can handle.

H) Does the goalie find it easy to concentrate?

The goalie should be able to concentrate with no difficulty because, during a game, when the puck is near his net, all his attention must be on the puck and he should be thinking only of what action he should take.
Try to notice if your young goalie pays attention when you speak to him and if he carries out your instructions quickly and correctly. Is he always in the middle of the action during training sessions and games, etc.?

Off-Ice Training

In North America, off-ice training is a relatively new type of training. A few years ago, it was used by only a few coaches.

By looking at new training methods developed in various countries around the world, it is easy to see that off-ice training is particularly good for the development of young players, especially beginner goalies.

This section will highlight the following topics:
— off-ice training sessions;
— group sports;
— individual sports;
— off-ice evaluation.

To ensure that the development of beginner goalies is as complete as possible, it is important to establish certain very specific rules, especially regarding the ideal frequency rate of off-ice training sessions and exercises.

	1	2	3	4
Period	Preseason	Season	Playoffs	Postseason
Month	J A	S O N D J F	M A	M J
A On-ice training				
B Off-ice training	F*: 4 times/ week 60 min. per training session 2 or 3 group sports 1 or 2 off-ice training sessions	F*: 1 times/week 90 min. per training session 1 off-ice training session	F*: nil	F*: 3-4 times/ week 60 min. per training session 1 or 2 group sports 1 or 2 individual sports

F*: Ideal frequency of off-ice training for beginner goalies in each of the various periods of a hockey season.

CHAPTER 4

OFF-ICE TRAINING SESSIONS

Summary

1. Highlight the importance of off-ice training for the beginner goalie.

2. List the physical qualities which should be developed during off-ice training sessions.

3. List the exercises designed to develop each of these physical qualities.

4. Outline a simple method to change the level of difficulty involved in each exercise.

5. Explain the periods included in an off-ice training session.

	1	2	3	4
Period	Preseason	Season	Playoffs	Postseason
Month	J A	S O N D J F	M A	M J
A **On-ice** **training**				
B **Off-ice** **training**	I — Off-ice training sessions			

From the start of July to the end of March (during the preseason and season), it is very useful for the beginning goalie to attend off-ice training sessions.

Held once or twice a week during the preseason and once a week during the season, the sessions should last approximately 60 minutes.

An off-ice training session should be composed of general physical development exercises — with the objective of increasing the beginner goalie's physical resources — used to develop the following physical qualities:

— speed
— agility
— flexibility

— strength
— endurance
— balance
— coordination

Exercises designed to develop speed

1. On a signal from the coach, over a distance of 15 feet (4.5 m) run forward, backward, side to side.

2. Positioning balls to create different courses. The goalie can begin in a standing position, lying on his stomach or lying on his back.

3. A quick back and forth race over a distance of 30, 65 or 100 feet (10, 20 30 m). Goalies should run forward, backward and side to side.

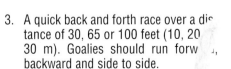

4. Run around a series of obstacles at full speed.

5. Run around a series of obstacles at full speed, also running around each individual obstacle.

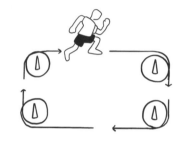

6. Run around a series of obstacles in a zigzag pattern.

a)

7. Run through a series of obstacles by circling each individual obstacle and returning to the starting point.

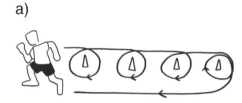

b)

8. On a signal from the coach, one of two goalies must try to take possession of a ball, starting from different positions.

b)

a)

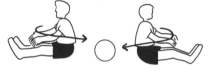

c)

9. Run in place as fast as you can.

10. Run at different speeds.
For example:
a) — 30 feet (10 m) at 100% of full speed
   — 30 feet (10 m) at 50% of full speed
   — 30 feet (10 m) at 100% of full speed
   — 30 feet (10 m) at 25% of full speed

b) — 30 feet (10 m) at 25% of full speed
   — 100 feet (30 m) at 50% of full speed
   — 65 feet (20 m) at 100% of full speed
   — 30 feet (10 m) at 25% of the full speed

11. Run while gradually increasing your speed, reaching full speed after 320 feet (100 m).

12. Run back and forth over various distances:
    a) 16 feet (5 m)
    b) 30 feet (10 m)
    c) 50 feet (15 m)
    d) 65 feet (20 m)
    e) 80 feet (25 m)
    f) 100 feet (30 m)

13. Jump rope as fast as possible.

14. Try to touch a partner within a restricted space (10 feet by 10 feet/3 m by 3 m).

15. Run on a steep incline.

16. Walk; on a signal, make a very quick start, run over a distance of 10 feet (3 m), then begin walking again.

17. Crouching, on a signal make a very quick start and run over a distance of 10, 16 or 30 feet (3, 5 or 10 m).

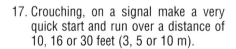

18. Walk behind a partner. On a signal, move ahead of him at full speed. Walk until the coach gives a second signal, and repeat the process.

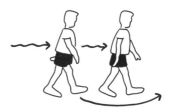

19. Standing, on a signal bend forward and touch the floor as quickly as possible.

20. Two partners are seated on the floor, with arms in the air. On a signal, each tries to grab the stick positioned between them.

21. Run and throw a ball through a hoop. Come back to the starting point and repeat the process using another ball.

22. On a signal, touch an object indicated by the coach and come back to the starting point as quickly as possible.

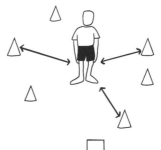

23. On a signal, change chairs quickly.

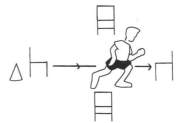

97

24. In a restricted space, one of two partners tries to avoid being touched by the other partner's hands.

25. One of two partners jumps to avoid the other partner's stick.

Exercises to develop agility

1. Alternately, touch each of two cones several times in a row.

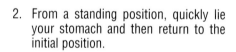

2. From a standing position, quickly lie your stomach and then return to the initial position.

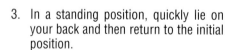

3. In a standing position, quickly lie on your back and then return to the initial position.

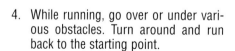

4. While running, go over or under various obstacles. Turn around and run back to the starting point.

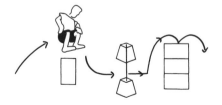

5. Move through a partner's legs very quickly. Run over a distance of 16 feet (5 m), then stop to let your partner do the same move.

6. Play leapfrog.

7. Run and respond to a coach's instructions. For example: sit down, roll over, go down on all fours, lie on your stomach, lie on your back, kneel, etc., then stand quickly and continue running.

8. Do a forward somersault, a backward somersault and leap forward.

9. Lie on your back, stand quickly and leap forward.

10. Lie on your stomach, stand quickly and make a forward somersault.

11. Standing, crouch down, leap forward and make a forward somersault.

12. Run with a ball in your hands and make a forward somersault.

13. Stand on a bench, jump forward to the floor and do a forward somersault.

14. Stand on a bench, jump backward to the floor and do a backward somersault.

15. Jump over a partner crouched on the floor and then roll.

16. Run quickly between obstacles positioned very close to one another.

17. Standing, touch your right heel very quickly and return to your initial position. Repeat touching the left heel.

18. From a crouching position, sit, lie on your stomach, stand, crouch, etc.

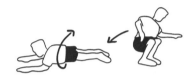

19. Standing, bring one knee to the floor and return to the initial position.

20. Standing, put both knees on the floor and return to the initial position.

Exercises to develop flexibility
Neck:

1. Lie on your back, lift your head toward your chest.

2. Lie on your stomach, lift your head toward your back.

3. Standing, turn your head to each side, as far as you can.

101

4. Standing, rotate your head in a full circle.

Shoulders:

5. Standing, bring your hands together behind your back.

6. Standing, make large circles with your arms, moving them forward and backward.

7. Bend your torso forward and lift your arms behind your back, pointing them toward the ceiling.

8. Standing, bring your arms in front of your body and make large circles, turning your arms clockwise and counterclockwise.

9. With a partner's help, bring your arms behind your body, as far as you can.

Torso:

10. Sitting on the floor, arms straight out to the sides, rotate your torso.

11. Standing, bend your torso forward, arms straight out to the sides, rotate your torso.

12. On all fours, arch your back and then create a hollow in the small of your back.

13. Standing, left hand on your hip and right hand behind your back, bend your torso toward the left. Bend toward the right. Repeat.

14. Lying on your stomach, hands behind your head, lift your torso off the floor, relax, lift your hips off the floor.

15. Two by two, torso bent forward, grab your partner's shoulders with your hands. Press downward to create a hollow in the small of your back.

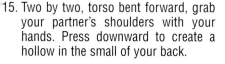

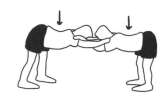

Hips:

16. Two by two, apply pressure to the back of the person seated on the floor, in front of you.

17. Two by two, lie on the floor holding each other's hands, swing your legs from one side of your body to the other.

18. Standing, arms stretched out to the sides, bring your left foot up to your right hand.

19. Crouching, with both hands on the floor, make a wide circle with one leg.

20. Crouching, with both hands on the floor, alternately stretch out one leg to the side of your body.

21. Sitting cross-legged, push your knees towards the floor.

22. Two by two, have your partner hold one of your feet while you bend to touch the ground with both hands.

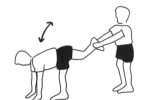

Legs:

23. Crouch and straighten your legs while keeping your hands on the floor.

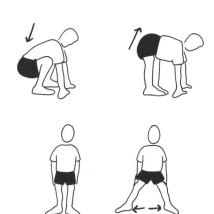

24. Standing, slowly spread your legs to the sides and then return to the initial position.

25. Sitting on the floor, bend your head toward your knees.

26. With one knee on the floor and the opposite leg stretched out, bend your torso forward to touch your foot with your hands.

27. Lying on your back, use your hand to lift one leg toward your torso.

28. With both hands on the floor, do a split.

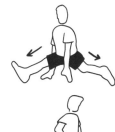

29. Standing, rotate your knees.

30. Standing, place the sole of your foot on a block of wood and lift an lower your heel.

Exercises to develop power

1. Jump as high as you can.

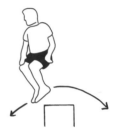

2. Jump over a bench, feet held together.

3. Jump as high as you can while doing different moves:
a) bend your legs;
b) point your legs and arms toward the back of your body;
c) point your legs to each side of your body.

a)

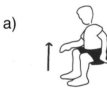

b)

c)

4. Crouching, leap as far forward as possible and stop in a crouch.

5. Leap onto a bench. Jump backward off the bench. As soon as your feet hit the ground, jump back onto the bench.

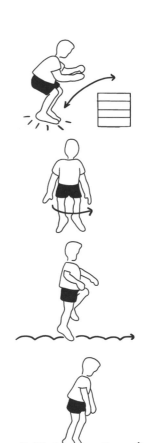

6. Jump up and down and make a $1/4$, $1/2$ and full turn.

7. Jump up and down on one leg.

8. Jump up and down with your feet held together.

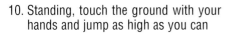

9. Run, using very long strides.

10. Standing, touch the ground with your hands and jump as high as you can

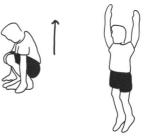

11. Crouching with a ball in your hands, leap forward and throw it as far as you can.

12. Do a Russian dance: crouching, extend your right leg to the side, bring it back, repeat with your left leg.

13. Push your partner forward as he tries to resist.

14. Run quickly over a distance of 16 feet (5 m) and do a long jump.

15. Move forward with your feet held together, as if you were skiing (slalom)

16. With your feet held together, jump up three steps at a time.

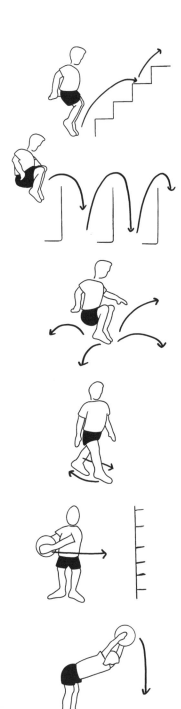

17. With your feet held together, jump over hurdles.

18. Leap in different directions.

19. Standing, place one foot in front of the other. Jump as you switch the forward foot.

20. Using both hands, throw a medicine ball as hard as you can.

21. Throw a medicine ball to the floor, as hard as you can.

22. Throw a medicine ball against the wall, as hard as you can.

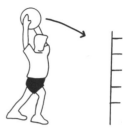

23. Two by two, with both feet, hit the ball as hard as you can.

Exercises to develop strength

1. Do pushups with your torso pointed toward the floor.

2. Do pushups with your torso pointed toward the ceiling.

3. Do situps.

4. Do knee bends.

5. Walk carrying a partner on your back.

6. Two by two, do the wheelbarrow move.

7. Carrying 15- to 20-pound (7- to 9-kg) weight, run over a distance of 65 to 100 feet (20 to 30 m).

8. Play tug of war with a partner.

9. Climb a rope.

10. With a partner's help, do leg lifts.

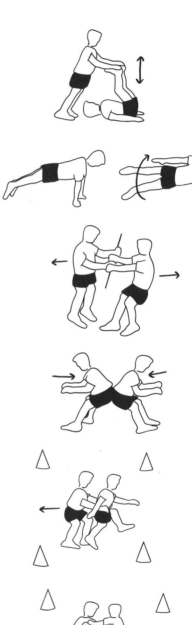

11. In a pushup position, rotate your body and lift one hand and one foot from the floor.

12. Two by two, try to snatch a stick from your partner's hands.

13. Back to back, push against your partner.

14. Hold back your partner as he tries to move out of a restricted space.

15. Try to push your partner out of a restricted space as he resists.

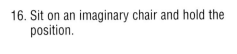

16. Sit on an imaginary chair and hold the position.

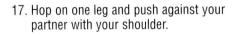

17. Hop on one leg and push against your partner with your shoulder.

18. Pull your partner by the arm.

19. Push against a wall.

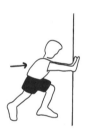

20. Hold a medicine ball between your feet and move it:
    a) from left to right;
    b) up and down;
    c) backward and forward

a)

b)

c)

21. Snatch a ball from your partner's hands.

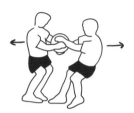

22. Lift your partner off the floor and put him down.

23. Stretch your back backwards.

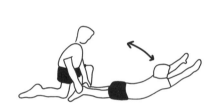

24. Throw a medicine ball as high as you can.

25. You can create a circuit:
— choose 10 exercises to develop different parts of the body;
— beginning with the first exercise, repeat each exercise quickly over a period of 30 seconds;
— rest for 30 seconds;
— move on to the next exercise.

Exercises to develop endurance

1. Run in place. Lift your knees very high and run for three to five minutes.

2. Run for 5 to 10 minutes. Your heart rate should increase to approximately 140 beats/minute.

3. Run quickly for 20 to 30 seconds. Rest for 40 to 60 seconds. Repeat several times.

4. Walk very quickly over a hilly course.

5. Play one-on-one soccer in a gym.

6. Any other exercise involving significant movement over a prolonged period of time. In this regard, exercises to develop speed and agility are excellent choices.

Exercises to develop balance

1. Standing, lift one leg to the side and make large circles.

2. Standing, lift one leg to the front of your body. Close your eyes and swing your arms forward and backward.

3. Standing, stretch one leg behind your body and bend forward to touch the ground with your hands. Bring your arms in line with the leg stretched out behind you. Return to your initial position.

4. Standing on two medicine balls:
   a) crouch and stand again;
   b) imitate puck stopping gestures with your hands.

a)

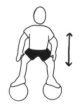

b)

5. Standing on a medicine ball:
   a) keep one or both feet on the ball;
   b) crouch and stand again;
   c) turn in a circle.

 a)   b)   c)

6. Place a plank on a medicine ball and stand on it.

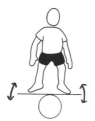

7. Do a head stand and keep your balance.

8. On the tips of your toes, go from a crouching position to a standing position, swinging your arms forward and backward. Return to your original position.

9. Hop on one foot, directly on marks on the floor. When you get to a mark, balance on it for three seconds before moving on to the next mark.

10. Standing, arms stretched out to the sides and eyes closed, touch your right hand with your left foot.

11. Sitting on the floor, with only your bottom touching the floor make a pedaling movement with your feet.

12. Standing, one leg stretched out toward the front of your body, crouch and then return to the initial position.

13. Standing on the tips of your toes, swing one leg from the front to the back of your body:
    a) with your eyes open;
    b) with your eyes closed.

14. Standing, place one foot against the knee of your opposite leg. Do the movement with hands on hips:
    a) with your eyes open;
    b) with your eyes closed.

15. Crouched and bent forward, place both hands on the floor. Rock forward, rest your knees against your elbows and lift your feet from the floor.

16. Standing on one foot, hands behind your back, hop between two out-stretched ropes without touching them.

17. Crouching, hands behind your back, make three small hops forward. Stay in place for three seconds, then:
    — hop backward three times;
    — hop to the right three times;
    — hop to the left three times.

18. Standing, place one finger on the floor and, using your finger as the anchoring point, turn in a circle five times. Stand, wait three seconds and walk in a straight line.

19. Run and using only one foot, jump through a hoop. With arms in the air, keep your balance for five seconds.

20. Standing, one foot on a block of wood 4 to 8 inches (10 to 20 cm) thick, hop from one foot to the other.

21. Standing on a block of wood, hop and make a $1/4$, $1/2$ and full turn:
    a) with both feet on the block;
    b) with one foot on the block.

22. Standing, with one foot on a block of wood, bend forward and pick up a ball.

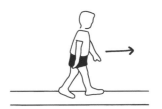

23. On a bench or low balance beam, walk:
    — forward;
    — backward;
    — sideways;
    — on the tips of your toes;
    — crouched;
    — at a running pace;
    — with a sandbag on your head;
    — with a sandbag on each hand, arms stretched out to the sides;
    — while dribbling a ball on the floor;
    — while catching balls thrown to you;
    — while juggling two balls;
    — while throwing and catching ball back and forth with a partner;
    — while hopping over medicine balls placed on the bench or beam.

Exercises to develop coordination

1. Run and use your feet to hit objects scattered on the floor.

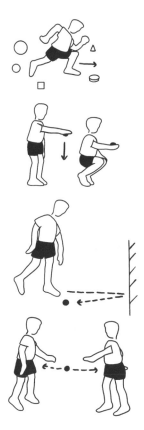

2. Standing, arms stretched out in front of your body, drop a ball and catch it before it touches the ground.

3. Kick a ball repeatedly against a wall.

4. Two by two, throw a ball back and forth:
   — directly;
   — with a bounce on the floor;
   — from far away;
   — from close up;
   — while advancing and backing away;
   — while turning in a circle once after each throw or catch.

5. Dribble a ball:
   — with one hand;
   — changing hands after each dribble;
   — standing
   — crouching;
   — kneeling;
   — walking;
   — in front of your body;
   — behind your body;
   — running;
   — using two balls.

121

6. Throw a ball repeatedly against a wall, as quickly as possible:
   — directly;
   — with a bounce;
   — throwing with one hand and catching with the other;
   — catching with both hands.

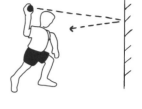

7. Two by two, take turns throwing a ball against a wall, as quickly as you can.

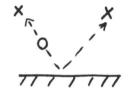

8. Dribble a basketball while looking ahead of you and:
   — walking;
   — running;
   — turning in a circle;
   — moving in a zigzag pattern.

9. Two by two, one player dribbles a ball and the other tries to take it away from him.

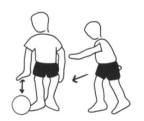

10. Throw a ball toward a target on a wall:
    — aiming above the target;
    — aiming to the right of the target;
    — aiming to the left of the target;
    — aiming below the target;
    — aiming at the middle of the target.

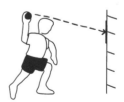

11. Throw balls or sandbags through hoops of different sizes, placed at different distances.

12. Run and jump into the air when you reach a specific spot.

13. Throw balls at targets placed at different heights.

14. Kick balls at targets placed at different heights.

15. Two by two, run in every direction while throwing a ball back and forth to each other.

16. Dribble a soccer ball with your feet, in as many different ways as you can.

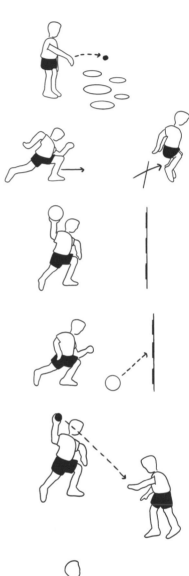

17. Throw a ball into the air. Turn around
    and catch the ball.

18. Hold a ball at arm's length, at shoulder
    height. Turn in a circle and catch the
    ball before it touches the floor.

19. Using a tennis racket or a baseball bat,
    throw balls:
    — different distances;
    — at different speeds;
    — at different heights.
You can also throw the balls:
    — with your hands;
    — with your feet.
Or you can:
    — cushion the ball;
    — catch the ball.

20. Two goalies face a wall. The coach
    throws a ball against the wall and calls
    out one goalie's name; that goalie
    must immediately grab the ball.

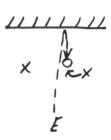

Note that physical qualities and the exercises they involve are not presented in any particular order of importance.

Each of the qualities described is important and should be developed, based on the potential of each beginner goalie.

The degree of difficulty involved in these exercises can be changed. In doing so, the coach's personality and creativity are called into play.

For example:
For balance exercise 4:
— stand on two medicine balloons.

And for coordination exercise 5:
— dribble a ball.

A whole new exercise can be created by combining the two exercises mentioned above:
— standing on two medicine balls, dribble a ball.
With the new exercise, the young goalie can develop both balance and coordination.

Another example:
Agility exercise 4:
— running, move over and under various obstacles.

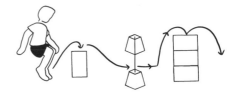

And power exercise 15:
— move forward with your feet held together, as if you were skiing (slalom).

By combining these two exercises, you get a second new exercise:
— Running, go over and under different obstacles. Come back to the starting point and move through the course again, with feet held together, as if you were skiing.

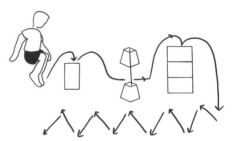

This exercise develops the goalie's agility and coordination.

As these two examples show, the coach can change the level of difficulty of exercises to develop more than one physical quality at the same time.
This series of exercises can help you:
— maintain your goalie's interest;
— adjust exercises to suit your goalie's potential;
— see your goalie's progress, if you're lucky enough to coach him for more than one season.

How to structure an off-ice training session

An off-ice training session includes three very specific periods:
1. the warm-up period;
2. the work period;
3. the cool-down period.

1. The warm-up period involves rotation exercises (neck, shoulders, torso, hips, knees, ankles), stretching (back, legs, groin, calves), jumping (on one foot, on both feet, in place, while moving, etc.), running in place and running over a distance.

2. The work stage involves general physical development exercises.
This period may include:
— exercises to develop only one physical quality;
— exercises to develop two or three physical qualities;
— exercises to develop several physical qualities.
The coach can choose the formula that best suits his goalie's needs.

3. The cool-down period is composed of group games, walking and relaxation exercises.

CHAPTER 5

GROUP SPORTS

SUMMARY

1. Demonstrate the importance of practicing group sports during the postseason and preseason.
2. Provide a list of the best sports from the training standpoint.

Group sports are very useful during the postseason and preseason.

They instill team spirit and competitiveness while keeping the young goalie physically fit.

During these two periods of the year, the beginner goalie should practice a group sport once or twice a week, one or two hours at a time.

The team sports that are most beneficial from the training standpoint are:
— soccer;
— handball;
— basketball;
— volleyball;
— baseball or softball (especially in the catcher's position);
— lacrosse;
— floor hockey;
— field hockey.

The hockey coach should strongly encourage his young goalies to practice a wide range of sports activities during the postseason and preseason periods, from early May to late August.

	1	2	3	4
Period	Preseason	Season	Playoffs	Postseason
Month	J A	S O N DJ F	M A	M J
A On-ice training				
B Off-ice training	II — Group sports ⊢————⊣			II — Group sports ⊢————⊣

CHAPTER 6

INDIVIDUAL SPORTS

SUMMARY

1. Demonstrate the importance of practicing individual sports during the postseason.

2. Provide a list of the individual sports best suited for this time of the year.

Individual sports should be practiced mainly during the postseason (although they are appropriate throughout the entire year).

The objective in the postseason period is to give the young goalie time to rest and relax, while staying physically fit.

To achieve this objective, the young goalie should practice high-energy individual sports twice or three times a week, for 60 minutes at a time.

The following activities are good choices:
— tennis;
— squash;
— racketball;
— ping-pong;
— skateboarding;
— bicycling;
— gymnastics;
— swimming.

	1	2	3	4
Period	Preseason	Season	Playoffs	Postseason
Month	J A	S O N D J F	M A	M J
A **On-ice** **training**				
B **Off-ice** **training**				III — Individual sports

CHAPTER 7

OFF-ICE EVALUATION

Summary

1. Demonstrate the importance of off-ice evaluation in selecting beginner goalies.

2. Outline selected tests and the application procedures required for each test.

3. Provide an annual compilation sheet for off-ice evaluation tests.

	1	2	3	4
Period	Preseason	Season	Playoffs	Postseason
Month	J A	S O N D J F	M A	M J
A On-ice training				
B Off-ice training		IV — Off-ice evaluation ⊢—⊣ ⊢—⊣ ⊢—⊣		

Off-ice evaluation of goalies has the same objectives as those set for on-ice evaluation. The process of applying tests is similar in both cases.

On the other hand, these tests have the following advantages: they make it possible to detect specific physical qualities that are indispensable to any goalie, which means that the coach can determine each player's physical potential.

Using these tests the coach can also make a selection based on long-term development, instead of focusing solely on the next season.

In some instances, early in the season a beginner goalie who already has one or two seasons of experience with a team will have an edge over another candidate. However, if after applying off-ice tests the coach sees that the second goalie is potentially a stronger player than the first, this new factor should be included in his selection criteria.

Off-ice tests* include the following:

A — Overall speed
B — Overall agility
C — Muscle strength
D — Flexibility of movement
E — Hip and back flexibility
F — Hand—eye coordination

---

* Most of these tests have been featured in a number of publications focusing on evaluation and, for the most part, they have been validated and confirmed. All of the tests featured here are drawn from Rémi Bissonnette, L'évaluation en éducation physique (Sherbrooke, PQ: University of Sherbrooke, 1977).

A — Overall speed

1. Definition:
Quality enabling the goalie to make one or several similar movements quickly, within a specific unit of time.

2. Material required:
— 1 pencil
— 1 result sheet
— 1 or 2 stopwatches
— 1 tape measure

3. Goalie's clothing:
— running shoes
— shorts
— sweatshirt

4. Procedure:
— The goalie stands at the starting line. His entire body should be behind the line.
— On a signal, the goalie runs to the finish line. When the player crosses the finish line, the stopwatch is stopped and results are noted immediately.

— Make sure the player warms up properly before taking the test.
— You should have two stopwatches on hand.
— Time is recorded to the nearest second.

B — Overall agility

1. Definition:
The ability of the body or parts of the body to change direction quickly and precisely.

2. Material required:
— 1 result sheet
— 1 pencil
— 1 tape measure
— 6 traffic cones
— gymnasium

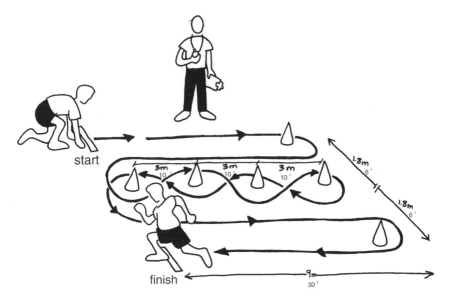

3. Goalie's clothing: See Test A.

4. Procedure:
— The subject lies on his stomach. His hands and forehead should be behind the starting line.
— On a signal, the goalie gets up and the stopwatch is started. The player runs through the course at full speed. When he crosses the finish line, the stopwatch is stopped. Results are noted immediately.
— Make sure the player warms up properly before taking the test.
— You should have two stopwatches on hand.
— Time is recorded to the nearest second.

C — Muscle strength

1. Definition:
Ability to show maximum muscle strength at maximum speed.

2. Material required:
— 1 tape measure
— 1 result sheet
— 1 pencil
— 1 felt-tip pen
— 1 roll of tape
— 15 feet (4.5 m)

3. Goalie's clothing: See Test A.

4. Procedure:
— The player stands behind the starting line, feet slightly apart.
— When the player is ready, he bends his knees, swings his arms back and forth a few times, then stretches his legs to jump as far as he can.
— The player must land on his feet and should avoid moving backward or placing one hand on the floor behind him.
— The coach measures the distance between the starting line and the location closest to where the player has landed (usually the spot where his heel has landed).
— The player has three tries and the best result is recorded.
— Distance is calculated to the nearest inch (cm).

D — Flexibility of movement

1. Definition:
Ability to repeat quickly a series of flex movements involving significant muscle elasticity, muscle stretching and recovery time.

2. Material required:
— 1 result sheet
— 1 pencil
— 1 roll of tape (to make Xs on the floor and wall)
— a wall 6 feet (1.8 m) in height

3. Goalie's clothing: See Test A.

4. Procedure:
— The subject stands with his back to the wall (12 to 18 inches/30 to 45 cm from the wall), feet a shoulder-width apart and hands resting on his thighs.

— On a signal, the player bends his torso forward, touches the X at his feet with his joined hands, straightens, turns left and touches the X on the wall. He repeats the full cycle. The goalie must repeat the cycle as often as possible within 20 seconds.
— The recorded result is the number of cycles repeated within 20 seconds.

E — Hip and back flexibility

1. Definition:
Range of movement in a joint.

2. Material required:
— 1 result sheet
— 1 pencil
— 1 box
— 1 20-inch (50-cm) ruler

3. Goalie's clothing: See Test A.

4. Procedure:
— The player sits on the floor and places his feet on the side of the box.
— With his legs stretched out straight along the floor, he stretches his hands forward and tries to touch as far up as possible on the ruler positioned perpendicular to the box.
— Make sure the player warms up properly before taking the test (particularly muscles in the back of the thigh).
— The result is recorded to the nearest centimetre.

F — Hand-eye coordination

1. Definition:
Ability to throw and catch objects.

2. Material required:
— 1 result sheet
— 1 pencil
— 1 stopwatch
— 1 roll of tape
— a wall and 20-foot (6-m) area
— 1 average-size rubber ball (e.g.: a field hockey ball)
— 1 20-inch (50-cm) ruler

3. Goalie's clothing: See Test A.

4. Procedure:
— The player stands behind a boundary line.
— On a signal, the player throws the ball at the wall, catches it when it rebounds and throws it again as quickly as possible in 30 seconds.
— The recorded result is the number of catches he makes.
— If the ball goes past him or doesn't rebound close enough to him, the test is done over again. On the second attempt, the goalie must retrieve the ball, return behind the boundary line and continue the test.

Annual Compilation Sheet for Off-Ice Evaluation Tests

Team: Date:			1st evaluation			
Names	Test A	Test B	Test C	Test D	Test E	Test F
1 —						
2 —						
3 —						
4 —						
5 —						
6 —						
Date:			2nd evaluation			
Names	Test A	Test B	Test C	Test D	Test E	Test F
1 —						
2 —						
3 —						
4 —						
5 —						
6 —						
Date:			3rd evaluation			
Names	Test A	Test B	Test C	Test D	Test E	Test F
1 —						
2 —						
3 —						
4 —						
5 —						
6 —						

The Coach's Work with the Goalie

CHAPTER
8

OBSERVATION
AND COMMUNICATION
WITH THE GOALIE

SUMMARY

1. Outline the objectives of observing beginner goalies.

2. Explain one type of observation and provide a corresponding form.

3. Describe a few principles needed for effective communication between the coach and the goalie.

4. Provide a table showing the various means of communication.

A — Observing the goalie

Observation is usually described as paying attention to specific aspects of the goalie's playing. Since a coach must give all his players equal attention, he should observe his goalies during practice sessions and games, just as he observes all his other players.

The objective of observation is to get to know goalies:

a) from the athletic standpoint (skills acquired and not acquired);
b) from the attitude standpoint (reaction to competitive situations, relationships with other players, with coaches, etc.).

Overall observation

This type of observation is used mainly during the season, during games.

The observation sheets provided in this chapter are very useful for:

— compiling shots on goal (for example: 9SI means that Number 9 on the opposing team made a slapshot goal);
— compiling goals not stopped by the goalie (for example: 4W means that Number 4 on the opposing team made a wrist shot and scored a goal);
— indicating the location where goals were scored (point at which they went into the net);
— indicating the total number of shots, saves, rebounds and goals in the period;
— noting various observations on the opposing team's play;
— noting observations on game situations that preceded goals scored against the goalie;
— showing statistics that can be useful to the coach;
— indicating the goalie's name, the period, the date and the opposing team.

Game Observation Sheet

Goalie: _____   Home team: _____

Period: _____   Visiting team: _____

Date: _____

Player No.:

Sweep shot: Sw

Wrist shot: W

Slap shot: SI

Backhand shot: B

Rebound shot: *

Goal: o

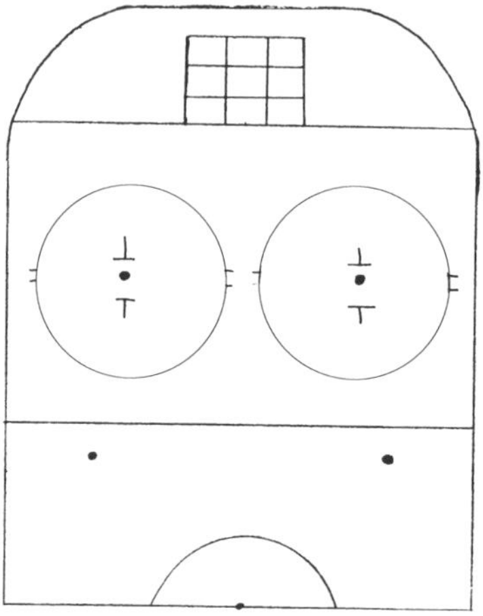

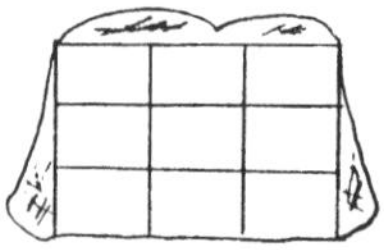

Indicate where the goal
was scored

Total shots: _____

Total saves: _____

Total rebounds: _____

Total goals: _____

Other observations:

_____

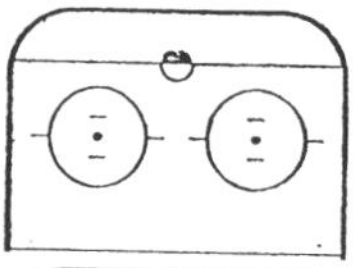

_____

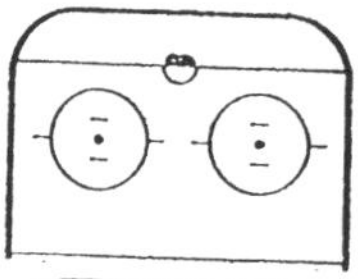

_____

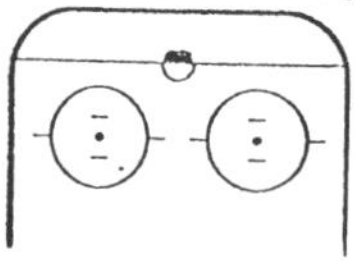

_____

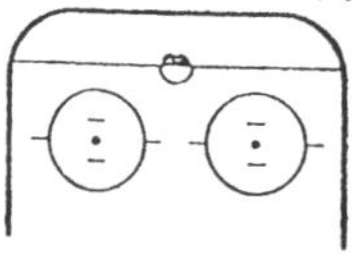

_____

_____

_____

_____

Sample Game Observation Sheet

Goalie: John

Period: 2nd

Home team: Blueville

Visiting team: Redville

Date: 22/11/94

Indicate where the goal was scored

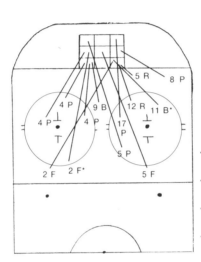

Player No.:

Sweep shot: Sw

Wrist shot: W

Slap shot: Sl

Backhand shot: B

Rebound shot*

Goal: o

Total shots: 12

Total saves: 10

Total rebounds: 2

Total goals: 2

Other observations:

The opposing team often makes backhand passes before shooting on the goal.

The power play is based on shots from...

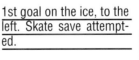

1st goal on the ice, to the left. Skate save attempted.

2nd goal, the goalie was badly positioned in front of the offense player

B — Communicating with goalies

Communication is defined as the transfer of information from one person (the coach) to another (the goalie).

Effective communication between the coach and the goalie is of vital importance.

Even if the coach is perfectly aware of his goalie's problems (and possible solutions), he will never be able to improve his players if he cannot communicate properly with them.

To communicate with beginner goalies, the coach should follow a few basic principles.

1. Make sure you use language that can be understood by a child of 8 to 12 years old. Explaining a technique with convoluted sentences filled with jargon is a waste of time if what you're saying has no real meaning for the young goalie. Instead, try to use simple and direct sentences with imagery to clarify your point.

2. At all times, remember to point out the link between the new elements you are introducing and elements that the goalie is already familiar with (things he has experienced firsthand); this will indicate to young goalies that your actions are progressive (and will progress throughout the season).

3. Speak at a speed that is appropriate to the complexity or unfamiliarity of the topic you are discussing. If the topic is easy to understand and familiar to the goalie, you can speak quickly. On the other hand, if the topic is completely new or seems to be relatively complex, speak more slowly.

4. Repeat the message as many times as necessary, in different ways.

The coach must remember to repeat messages so that they are well understood by the young goalie.

Repetition is essential to a good understanding of the message.

A good way to check if the message has been grasped by the young goalie is to have him repeat, in his own words, what the coach has communicated to him.

The following diagram shows a successful communication between a coach and a goalie.

Diagram showing effective communication between a coach and a goalie

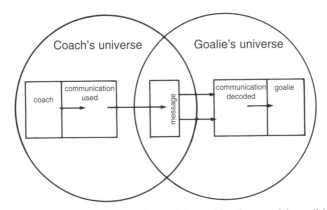

Diagram I: Note that the message is simultaneously part of the coach's universe and the goalie's universe. Therefore, the message complies with the principles outlined previously. The communication is successful.

If, on the other hand, the communication used by the coach does not comply with one or more of the principles outlined previously, most probably the message will not be understood by the goalie.

Diagram showing inadequate communication

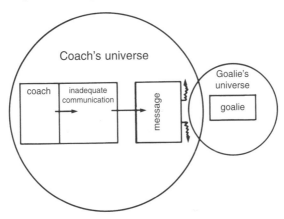

Diagram II: The message does not comply with certain communication principles and cannot penetrate into the goalie's universe. Therefore, the communication is inadequate.

Means of communication

The coach can choose from a wide range of means of communication. Usually, the right choice of one or several of these means leads to effective communication between the coach and his goalies.

147

Examples of different types of communication

1 — Verbal communication

Verbal exchange between the coach and his goalies.

2 — Graphic communication

Verbal exchange between the coach and his goalies.

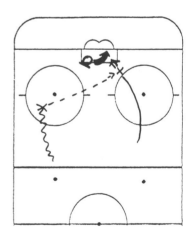

3 — Communication through imagery

Photos from books or newspapers, hockey card drawings, etc.

4 — Written communication

Written description of a technical move, point by point.

The basic kneeling position

1. Pads must be spread out to the sides of the body as far as they will go, touching the ice surface on their entire length.
2. The torso is straight and the bottom is lifted to cover as much space as possible toward the top of the net. The head is held high to keep a close watch on the game.
3. Gloves are positioned to each side of the body.
4. The stick, held at an angle to send pucks into the corner of the rink, is positioned directly in front of the opening between the legs.
5. The body's weight is shifted onto the knees.

5 — Statistical communication

Statistics taken from game observation sheets.
Examples:
— number of goals per game;
— number of shots/number of goals;
— number of shots/number of rebounds;
— number of goals in the upper, middle and lower portions of the net/number of shots in the upper, middle and lower portions of the net

6 — Audiovisual communication

Audiovisual tapes of training sessions and games.

7 — Multiple communication

The simultaneous use of two, three or four types of communication.

CHAPTER
9

CORRECTING
BEGINNER
GOALIES

SUMMARY

1. Outline an effective and progressive teaching approach for correcting beginner goalies.

2. Describe a few important points to highlight when correcting beginner goalies.

In addition to providing exercises designed to help the goalie learn skating techniques (Chapter 1) and basic techniques (Chapter 2), at times the coach must correct his goalies.

Normally, specific correction exercises should never be introduced early in the season. Instead, the coach should observe goalies during training camp and the during the first month of the regular season.*

This approach is the only logical option. How can you correct a goalie if you still don't know what his strong and weak points are?

Many coaches believe that a goalie is harder to correct than an offense player is. Luckily, this particular myth seems to be fading away.

Correcting a goalie simply requires compliance with a few steps in the teaching process.

Suggested teaching steps

Step 1

The coach must create a climate of trust between himself and his goalie.

To do so, corrections should never be made at random. Instead, the coach should demonstrate for the goalie (with proof in the form of written notes or coded observations) that he shows a real and frequent weakness.

The goalie must be made aware of the problem before beginning correction exercises.

Example for Step 1

The coach points out to his goalie that, during previous games, the goalie had eight chances to move to block a corner shot on goal and at no time did he make the right move. Observation sheets from previous games are used as proof.

153

---

* The chapter on observation and communication with goalies explains a few observation methods (see Chapter 8).

Step 2

The coach should explain the technical move using different types of communication (see Chapter 8).

This step is absolutely essential for the goalie to become mentally aware of the mechanics of the move.

Examples for Step 2

1. The coach shows a picture of a goalie making a move to block a corner shot.

2. The major technical aspects of the move are pointed out to the goalie.

3. A diagram of the play is used to describe the direction of the goalie's push-off.

Step 3

The coach must develop one or more specific correction exercises. The exercises will be used to show the goalie how to make the move properly, as opposed to how he has been making the move until now.

The exercises should be repeated several times. On the one hand, repetitions serve to make the goalie physically aware of the mechanics of the move and, on the other, he becomes fully familiar with the move.

Examples for Step 3

The coach develops a few specific correction exercises.

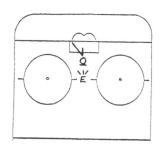

On the coach's signal, in his net the goalie moves from one goal post to the slot.

Step 4

The coach must create a game situation (as real as possible) where the goalie may be tempted to repeat the faulty move the coach wants to correct.

This step must be repeated until the goalie has developed a new automatic reaction. If not, the new move will disappear as soon as the goalie is in a stressful situation (for example, during an important game).

Examples for Step 4

The trainer develops correction exercises that resemble game situations.

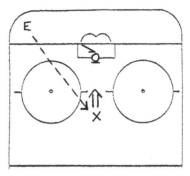

A pass from a corner for a shot on goal from the slot.

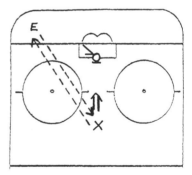

The player who is in front of the net passes the puck to the coach, who is in the corner of the rink. When the coach has the puck, he shoots it to the player in the slot, who makes a shot on goal.

A few important points to remember when developing correction exercises

— Correct only one or two problems at a time.

— Be aware of the goalie's learning ability and don't go from one step to the next too quickly. Be patient — patience pays off in the long run.

— Correction exercises should make up no more than 10 to 15% of the total time used for on-ice training. The remaining time should be used for skating exercises, practicing basic techniques, shooting and simulating plays.

— The correction exercises should be geared to the goalie's speed. (For example: when two or three players pass the puck, can the goalie move about fast enough?)

— The exercise should be geared to the goalie's speed of recovery. (For example: does the goalie have enough time to get up from the ice when another forward advances on the net?)

— The goalie's success ratio should be in the order of 6 to 8 successful attempts out of a total of 10 tries. If not, the correction exercise is too fast or too complex for him.

— Be careful when correcting your goalie; if the goalie is not prepared before corrections are made or if corrections are negative, he will probably show a noticeable drop in performance levels.

— Never make corrections the day before a game. Doing so will have the effect of putting doubt in the goalie's mind and, as a result, his personal preparation will suffer. Instead, wait until the next training session to talk to your goalie.

— The number of shots on goal during a training session is not the only factor that will determine a goalie's success.

CHAPTER 10

THE ROLE OF A
GOALTENDING COACH

Summary

1. Outline the four types of situations that call for the goaltending coach's intervention.

2. Briefly describe the roles of a goaltending coach during on-ice training sessions.

3. Briefly describe the roles of a goaltending coach during off-ice training sessions.

4. Briefly describe the roles of a goaltending coach during games.

5. Briefly describe the roles of a goaltending coach during his own personal preparation.

There can be no doubt that a head coach can't train his two goalies as effectively as he would if he was assisted by a coach assigned specifically to them.

In the past few years, an increasing number of teams at all levels are including such specialists on their roster. The effort is praiseworthy, but in many instances the goaltending coach is unable to justify his job.

This is due mainly to ignorance (on the part of the head coach or the goaltending specialist himself) of the roles the goaltending coach should play when dealing with his goalies to create a climate favorable to the learning process.

This chapter provides a list of the roles played by a goaltending coach. They are not described in detail, since most roles can be adapted in different ways, depending on the category, coach, caliber of play, individual goalies, etc.

First, it is good to know that the goaltending coach should intervene in very specific types of situations, namely:
1. On-ice training
2. Off-ice training
3. Games
4. His own personal preparation

1. On-ice training sessions

During on-ice training sessions, the goaltending coach plays the following roles:

A — Observation of goalies

First and foremost, a coach who wants to make corrections and provide information to his goalies must be a good observer.

Various means of observing goalies are described in the chapter on observation (see Chapter 8).

B — Communication with goalies

The coach must be able to communicate the result of his observation to his goalies. This point is very important for goalies to be able to perceive their own difficulties and correct them.

In the chapter on communication, you will find various means to achieve effective communication (see Chapter 8).

C — Periodic evaluation of goalies

As it is in any other sport, detailed evaluation is crucial.

To do so, tests focusing on the technical aspects of the game can be carried out early in the season, at mid season and late in the season.

Several tests are described in the chapter on the subject (see Chapter 3).

D — Preparing and motivating goalies

Through his interventions, the coach must give his goalies positive preparation for training sessions and games. He must also create a climate that will give goalies the motivation to improve their skills.

E — Developing training sessions adapted to goalies

Training sessions must include exercises focusing on skating techniques, basic techniques and correction.

2. Off-ice training sessions

During off-ice training sessions, the goaltending coach plays the following roles:

A — Preparing training sessions during the preseason period

Off-ice training sessions during the preseason period must be designed to prepare the goalie adequately for the coming season.

For beginner goalies, this type of training is composed entirely of exercises focusing on overall physical development.

B — Preparing training sessions during the season

Off-ice training sessions during the season are aimed mainly at improving or maintaining the goalie's overall physical fitness level.

For beginner goalies, this type of training is not much different from preseason off-ice training (see Chapter 4).

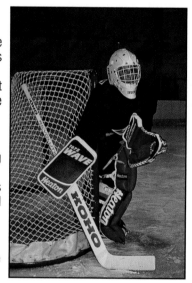

C — Periodic evaluation of goalies

Off-ice evaluation focuses mainly on determining the fitness level of the beginner goalie.

The chapter on off-ice evaluation describes tests that can be carried out early in the season, at mid season or late in the season (see Chapter 7).

3. Games

During games, the goaltending coach plays the following roles:

A — Selecting a beginner goalie

Given what his knows about his goalies, the coach must be able to determine which goalie is best for a particular game. Subsequently, he should communicate his decision to his head coach and his goalies.

Since the goalies involved are relatively young, at all costs you must give them the chance to play in games as often as possible. Various means of substitution can be used for beginner goalies:

— alternate between games
— alternate between periods
— alternate between half-periods
— alternate after every two or three line changes
— alternate after each goal
— alternate after every two goals

B — Preparing and motivating the starting and substitute goalie

Before a game, goaltending coaches can be called upon to play a role in the mental preparation of goalies.

To do so, take a close look at the following points:
— observation of the opposing team
— observation of the opposing players
— review of basic techniques
— review of specific game situations:
  • breakaways
  • 1 on 1 plays
  • 2 on 1 plays
  • 3 on 1 plays
  • 3 on 2 plays
— player behind the net
— statistics for the last game against the team
— any other topic deemed appropriate by the coach

C — Preparing a warm-up before parties

Warm-ups are very important because they give goalies the chance to practice the technical moves they will need during the game.

D — Observing the goalie during the game

As soon as the game begins, the goaltending coach should limit his role to that of an observer.

Various means of observation may be used (see Chapter 8).

E — Corrections and instructions during the game and between periods

Depending on the substitution method used, the coach can communicate with his goalies either during the game, or between periods only.

To be effective, he must have all pertinent information at hand to share with his goalies:
— record of shots
— players who shot on goal
— type of shots
— direction of shots, etc.
— particularly dangerous opposing players
— tactics used by the opposing team
— technical errors
— the goalie's good plays

F — Responsibility for making changes during the game

At times, the goaltending coach may be forced to make a goalie substitution. This decision is extremely complex since the effects of a bad decision can lead to a loss and can cause a negative reaction on the part of the goalie who is replaced.

Before making a substitution, the goalie should consider the following questions:

— Can the team still win the game?

— Is the goalie directly responsible for the goals scored against him?

— Can the goalie be affected psychologically if he is kept in the game or removed from it?

— Will the substitute goalie be an effective replacement?

G — Observing opposing goalies

The goaltending coach is the key person in this process, and during games he can observe the opposing goalie and communicate any weaknesses he sees to the head coach, who then communicates them to his forwards.

4. The coach's personal preparation

In large part, the coach's personal preparation determines the quality of his intervention with his goalies. Therefore, it is important for him to stay up-to-date on several files:

1. File on training sessions carried out since the beginning of the season:
   — on the ice
   — off the ice
2 File on recorded observations:
   — during training sessions
   — during games
3. File containing various statistics:
   — individual averages
   — team average
   — number of shots, saves and rebounds
   — number of goals, their location, types of shots
   — number of wins and losses
4. File containing evaluation test results:
   — on the ice
   — off the ice

Conclusion

*H*ockey Goaltending for Young Players is not intended as a rigid set of rules to be followed by trainers, parents and goalies. Instead, it is a reference work that they can consult and modify to meet their own particular needs.

Reading the advice contained in this book and applying it, even if only partially, will help make those involved in minor league hockey more aware of the importance of developing beginner goalies at the same pace as the team's other players.

In addition, the publication may lead to new ideas in an area of hockey that has gone unnoticed for far too long.

BIBLIOGRAPHY

A.H.A.U.S. *Coaching Youth Ice Hockey.* Chicago: The Athletic Institute, 1975.

BERTAGNA, Joseph. *Goaltending.* Cambridge, Mass.: Cosmos Presse Inc., 1976.

BISSONNETTE, Rémi. *Évaluation en éducation physique.* Sherbrooke: Faculty of Physical Education and Sports, University of Sherbrooke, 1977.

BOUCHARD, Claude, BRUNELLE, Jean, GODBOUT, Paul. *La valeur physique et le curriculum en éducation physique.* Quebec City: Édition du Pélican, 1973.

BOUCHARD, Claude, BRUNELLE, Jean, GODBOUT, Paul. *La préparation d'un champion.* Quebec City: Édition du Pélican, 1973.

BULLER, Bernard. *Selecting and Coaching the Goaltender.* Coaching Clinic, 1977.

CHAPLEAU, Claude, FRIGON, Piere, MARCOTTE, Gaston. *Les passes au hockey.* Montreal: Éditions de l'Homme, 1979.

CHILD, Murray, ARMSTRONG, Bert. *Goaltending Fundamentals.* Toronto: Hockey Ontario Development Committee, 1974.

DARMON, R.Y., LAROCHE, M., PETROF, J.V. *Le marketing, fondements et applications.* Montreal: McGraw-Hill, 1978.

DESROSIERS, Pauline, TOUSIGNANT, Marielle. *L'éducation physique à l'élémentaire.* Quebec City: Les Presses de l'Université Laval, 1977.

DIOTTE, Guy, RUEL, André. *Techniques du hockey en U.R.S.S.* Montreal: Éditions de l'Homme, 1976.

DRYDEN, Dave. *Coaching Goaltenders.* Edmonton: Capitals Sports Entreprises Ltd., 1976.

ELLSTRÖM, Sven Allan. *Malvaktsspel.* Sweden: Ceme-Forloget, 1979.

F.Q.H.G. *Manuel I, technique.* Montreal: Fédération québécoise de hockey sur glace, 1982.

GAGNON, Gérard. *Hockey, système de jeu et tactiques.* Montreal: Les Presses de l'Université de Montréal, 1983.

HENWOOD, Dale. *La position du gardien de but.* Ottawa: Séminaire du niveau V, 1981.

HORSKY, Ladislav. *Eishockey.* Germany: Wilhelmlimpet-Verlag, 1967.

HORSKY, Ladislav. *Telesna pripravo pohyblivost.* Kosice: T. J. USZ, 1975.

HORSKY, Ladislav. *Trenink Ledniko Hockeje.* Prague: Olympia, 1977.

KEITH, Forbes. *Off-Ice Conditioning Program for Hockey Goalkeepers.* Athletic Journal, 1976.

KOSTKA, Vladimir. *Formation des jeunes joueurs de hockey de la Tchécoslovaquie.* Ottawa: L'Association de hockey amateur (First edition: Prague, 1975).

LARIVIERE, Georges, BOURNIVAL, Justin. *Hockey the Right Start.* Toronto: Holt, Rinehart and Winston, 1969.

LARIVIERE, G., GODBOUT, P. *Mesure de la condition physique et de l'efficacité technique de joueurs de hockey sur glace.* Quebec City: Édition du Pélican, 1976.

LÜTSOLA, Seppo, HERKKILA, Lasse. *Manuel d'entrainement en terrain sec, méthode finlandaise.* Ottawa: Canadian Amateur Hockey Association.

MARCOTTE Gaston. *Évaluation technique du joueur de hockey.* Quebec City: Édition du Pélican, 1977.

MARCOTTE, Gaston, POIRIER, Gilles. *La préparation physique du joueur de hockey.* Quebec City: Édition du Pélican, 1978.

PELCHAT, Christian. *Fonction et rôle du gardien de but, Manuel grade III.* Montreal: Fédération de hockey sur glace du Québec, 1973.

PLANTE, Jacques. *Devant le filet.* Montreal: Les Éditions de l'Homme, 1972.

SHERO, Fred, BEAULIEU, André. *Hockey for the Coach, the Player and the Fan.* New York: Simon and Schuster, 1979.

TAYLOR, Joe. *Lloyd Percival's Total Conditioning for Hockey.* Don Mills: Fitzhenry and Whiteside, 1978.

VAIRO, Lou. *The A.H.A.U.S. Coaches Drill Book.* Colorado: Amateur Hockey Association of the United States, 1979.

VAN DER MAREN, Jean Marie. *La communication pédagogique: Éléments pour une didactique générale.* Apprentissage et socialisation, Vol. 1, No. 1, 1978.

WALFORD, Gerald H. *Ice Hockey: an Illustrated Guide for Coaches.* New York: Ronald Press Company, 1971.

Notes

Game Observation Sheet

Goalie: _____

Period: _____

Home team: _____

Visiting team: _____

Date: _____

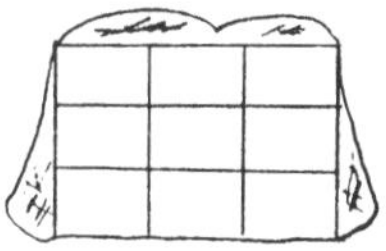

Player No:

Sweep shot: Sw

Wrist shot: W

Slap shot: Sl

Backhand shot: B

Rebound shot: *

Goal: o

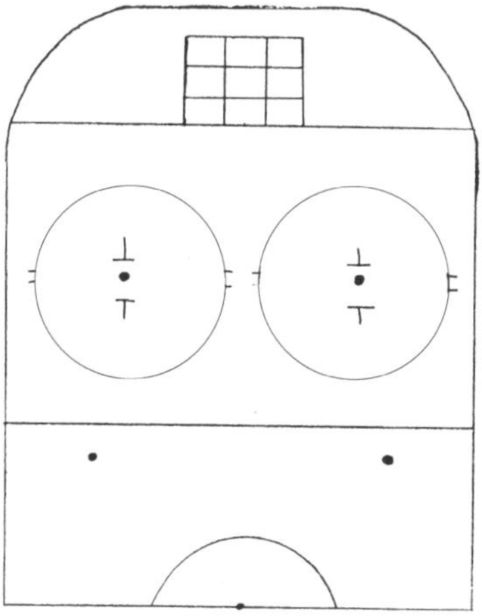

Indicate where the goal was scored

Total shots: _____

Total saves: _____

Total rebounds:_____

Total goals: _____

Other observations:

_____
_____
_____
_____

_____
_____
_____
_____

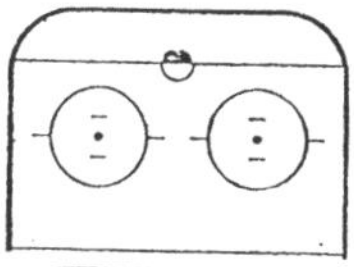

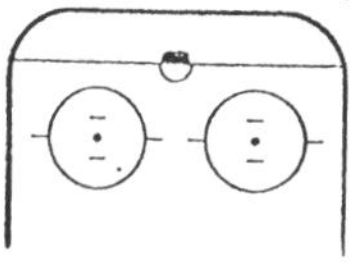

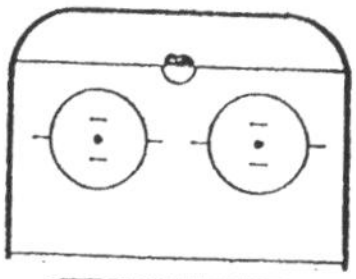

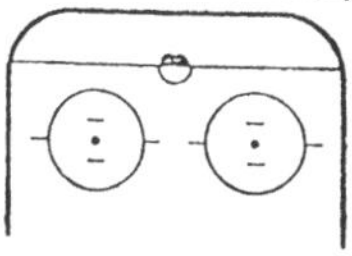

Notes

Game Observation Sheet

Goalie: _____

Period: _____

Home team: _____

Visiting team: _____

Date: _____

Player No:

Sweep shot: Sw

Wrist shot: W

Slap shot: Sl

Backhand shot: B

Rebound shot: *

Goal: o

Indicate where the goal was scored

Total shots: _____

Total saves: _____

Total rebounds: _____

Total goals: _____

Other observations:

_____

_____

_____

_____

_____

_____

_____

_____

Notes

Game Observation Sheet

Goalie: _____

Period: _____

Home team: _____

Visiting team: _____

Date: _____

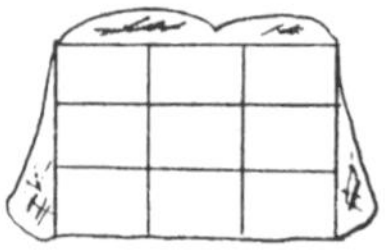

Player No:

Sweep shot: Sw

Wrist shot: W

Slap shot: Sl

Backhand shot: B

Rebound shot: *

Goal: o

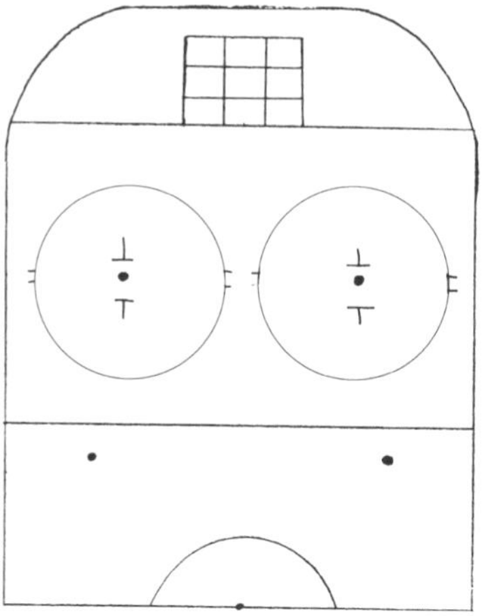

Indicate where the goal was scored

Total shots: _____

Total saves: _____

Total rebounds:_____

Total goals: _____

Other observations:

_____
_____
_____
_____

_____
_____
_____
_____

_____
_____
_____
_____

_____
_____
_____
_____

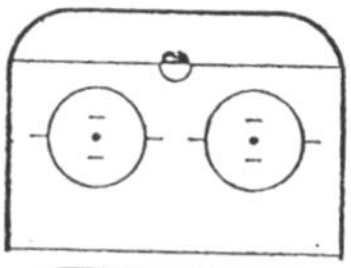

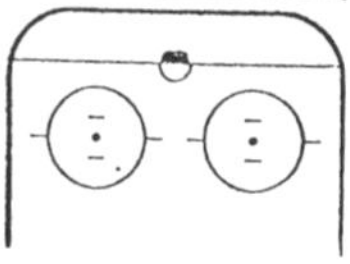

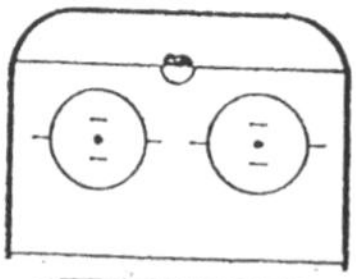

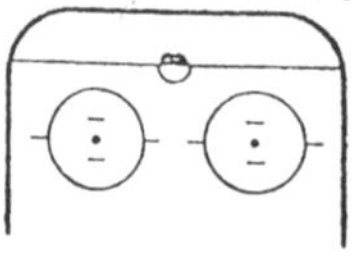

Notes

Notes

Printed in Canada